W9-CAE-097

Reporting
Research
in Psychology

 Sixth Edition

Reporting Research

in Psychology

How to Meet Journal Article Reporting Standards

Harris Cooper

American Psychological Association • *Washington, DC*

Copyright © 2011 by the American Psychological Association. All rights reserved. Except as permitted under the United States Copyright Act of 1976, no part of this publication may be reproduced or distributed in any form or by any means, including, but not limited to, the process of scanning and digitization, or stored in a database or retrieval system, without the prior written permission of the publisher.

Examples used throughout this volume from material copyrighted by the American Psychological Association have been adapted and reprinted with permission.

Published by
American Psychological Association
750 First Street, NE
Washington, DC 20002
www.apa.org

To order
APA Order Department
P.O. Box 92984
Washington, DC 20090-2984
Tel: (800) 374-2721; Direct: (202) 336-5510
Fax: (202) 336-5502; TDD/TTY: (202) 336-6123
Online: www.apa.org/pubs/books
E-mail: order@apa.org

In the U.K., Europe, Africa, and the Middle East, copies may be ordered from
American Psychological Association
3 Henrietta Street
Covent Garden, London
WC2E 8LU England

Typeset in Sabon, Futura, and Univers by Circle Graphics, Columbia, MD

Printer: United Book Press, Baltimore, MD
Cover Designer: Naylor Design, Washington, DC

The opinions and statements published are the responsibility of the authors, and such opinions and statements do not necessarily represent the policies of the American Psychological Association.

Library of Congress Cataloging-in-Publication Data

Cooper, Harris M.
   Reporting research in psychology : how to meet journal article reporting standards/
Harris Cooper. — 1st ed.
       p. cm.
   Includes bibliographical references and index.
   ISBN-13: 978-1-4338-0916-3
   ISBN-10: 1-4338-0916-8
   1. Psychology—Authorship—Style manuals. 2. Journalism—Style manuals. 3. Psychology—
Research—Handbooks, manuals, etc. 4. Report writing—Handbooks, manuals, etc.
5. Psychological literature—Publishing—Handbooks, manuals, etc. I. Title.
   BF76.8.C66 2011
   150.72'1—dc22
                                    2010024818

British Library Cataloguing-in-Publication Data
A CIP record is available from the British Library.

Printed in the United States of America
First Edition

Contents

Acknowledgments

I thank the coauthors of the American Psychological Association's Journal Article Reporting Standards (JARS) for their consent to rework report material for Chapters 1 and 7. I also thank Saiying Steenbergen-Hu and Amy Dent for providing me with comments on a draft of the book—as did Mary Lynn Skutley and Linda McCarter for Chapter 2—and the authors whose articles provide the examples that appear throughout the text.

Reporting
Research
in Psychology

Reporting Standards for Research in Psychology: Why Do We Need Them? What Might They Be?

Triple-Chocolate Layer Cake

Ingredients:

½ cup cold buttermilk

1 tablespoon instant espresso powder

2 teaspoons vanilla extract

1 cup cake flour

6 tablespoons unsweetened cocoa powder

½ teaspoon salt

¼ teaspoon baking powder

¼ teaspoon baking soda

3 large eggs

½ cup unsalted butter, room temperature

Instructions:

Preheat oven. Butter three 8-inch-diameter cake pans with 1-inch-high sides. Line bottom of three pans. Stir buttermilk, espresso powder, and vanilla until powder dissolves. Sift next five ingredients into large bowl. Add eggs and butter; beat until mixture is thick and smooth. Add buttermilk mixture; beat until light and fluffy. Divide batter among pans. Bake about 20 minutes.

Sound tasty? Problem is, I left sugar out of the list of ingredients (1¼ cups). What would chocolate cake taste like if the recipe left out sugar? And although I told you to preheat the oven, I forgot to say to what temperature (350 °F). If I didn't tell you what temperature to set the oven, what are the chances you could follow my recipe and make the cake? (Oops, those 1-inch-high pans should have been 1½ inches high; sorry for the mess.)

Why Are Journal Article Reporting Standards Needed?

In many ways, the report of a psychology research project contains a recipe. Without accurate descriptions of the ingredients (the manipulations and measures) and the instructions (research design and implementation), it is impossible for others to replicate what you have done.

Recently, there has been a growing sense in the social and behavioral sciences that the recipes contained in our research reports often do not serve us well. Recognizing this, the Publications and Communications Board of the American Psychological Association (APA) formed a group, called the Journal Article Reporting Standards Working Group (hereinafter the JARS Group), to look into the issue. The board wanted to learn about reporting standards that had been developed in fields related to psychology and how the issue of reporting standards might be handled in the sixth edition of the *Publication Manual of the American Psychological Association* (APA, 2010b; hereinafter the *Publication Manual*).

The Publications and Communications Board asked the JARS Group to look at existing reporting standards and adapt them for use by psychology researchers and other behavioral scientists, if this was desirable. The JARS Group was composed of five former editors of APA journals.[1] This book presents the reporting standards that came out of our effort, our recipe for how to create a good recipe, you might say. For a more in-depth description of why reporting standards are needed, what we found in the literature on this topic, and how the JARS Group went about constructing the JARS, see Chapter 7.

How to Use the JARS Tables

The tables and figure in Appendix 1.1 present the JARS, divided into four parts. First, Table A1.1 presents what the JARS recommends for inclusion in all reports on new data collections.[2] These all-purpose recommendations contain only a brief entry regarding the type of research design because social and behavioral scientists use so many different research designs and the JARS needs different items for each type of research design. Then, depending on the research design used, researchers pick the appropriate set of items (the JARS calls these modules) to be added to the all-purpose items.

Currently, the JARS provides reporting items for only one family of research designs; Table A1.2 provides reporting standards for research designs involving purposive or experimental manipulations or interventions. Table A1.3 provides separate items for reporting a study with a purposive manipulation that either (a) used random assign-

---

[1]The JARS Group was composed of Mark Appelbaum, Scott Maxwell, Arthur Stone, Kenneth J. Sher, and Harris Cooper. I served as chair.

[2]Of course, the JARS is an inanimate object so it does not actually recommend anything. However, I use the active voice for the JARS throughout the text for speedier exposition.

ment of participants to conditions (Module A1) or (b) used a procedure other than random assignment to assign participants to conditions (Module A2). The former type of design is referred to as an *experiment* when it is conducted in a laboratory—for example, when the label on a perfume bottle is varied to test the effects of different labels on the rated pleasantness of a fragrance (I use this hypothetical experiment throughout the text, along with some examples of real studies). When a study using random assignment is conducted in a nonlaboratory setting—for example, when a new type of therapy for depression is evaluated—the study often is referred to as a *randomized clinical trial*. Designs with purposive manipulations not involving random assignment are often referred to as *quasi-experiments*.

This modular approach makes it possible for other research designs to be added to the JARS by adding new modules.[3] As these standards are developed, they can be given different module labels (our label is "Reporting Standards for Studies With an Experimental Manipulation or Intervention") as well as their own submodules (in our case, "Studies Using Random Assignment" and "Studies Using Nonrandom Assignment"), depending on what is needed to fully capture the variations in that research design.

The specific items in each of the tables are categorized into the sections of a research report used in APA journals. To see how the tables would be used, note that the Method section in Table A1.1 is divided into subsections for participant characteristics, sampling procedures, sample size, measures and covariates, and an overall categorization of the research design. Then, Table A1.2 presents additional information that should be reported about the research design if the design being described involved a laboratory manipulation or intervention in a natural setting, including a description of the manipulation or intervention itself and the units of delivery and analysis. Next, Table A1.3 presents the sets of reporting standards to be used depending on whether the participants in the study were assigned to conditions with a random (Module A1) or nonrandom (Module A2) procedure.

Finally, Figure A1.1 provides an appealing device to present the flow of participants through the stages of a study with either random or nonrandom assignment. It is an adaptation of the chart recommended in the Consolidated Standards of Reporting Trials (CONSORT) guidelines (see Appendix 1.1). It details the amount and causes of participant loss (often called *attrition*) at each stage of the research, regardless of how condition assignment was accomplished. Therefore, it can be regarded as appropriate for use as part of either Module A1 or Module A2. This scheme may seem complex, but if you choose a design and work it through the tables, the logic becomes clear.

The Tension Between Complete Reporting and Space Limitations

A thought probably crossed your mind as you examined the entries in the JARS tables: "My goodness! How am I going to fit all of this information into a single report, especially given that the journal I want to submit my paper to has a page limit?"

---

[3]The JARS Group recognized that our work was incomplete because we included only one family of research designs. In the future, we hope (and expect) that new modules regarding other research designs will be added to the standards to be used in conjunction with Table A1.1. Also, additional standards could be adopted for any parts of a report (see, e.g., Davidson et al., 2003). In future revisions of the JARS (and this book), perhaps these will be added.

Good question. There is clearly a tension between transparency in reporting and the space limitations imposed by the print medium. As descriptions of research expand, so does the space needed to report them. However, not everything recommended in the JARS and in the Meta-Analysis Reporting Standards (MARS; see Chapter 6) needs to go into print. Recent improvements in the capacity of and access to electronic storage of information suggest that this trade-off could someday disappear. For example, APA journals, among others, now make available to authors online supplemental archives that can be used to store supplemental materials associated with the articles that appear in print (APA, 2010b, pp. 38–40, section 2.13, Appendices and Supplemental Materials). Similarly, it is possible for electronic journals to contain short reports of research with hot links to websites containing supplementary files.

Therefore, some of the information in the JARS and MARS might not appear in the published article itself but rather in an online supplemental archive available on the Internet. For example, if the instructions in your investigation were lengthy but critical to understanding what was done, they may be presented verbatim in an online supplemental archive. Supplemental materials might also include the flowchart of participants through the study. It might include oversized tables of results (especially those associated with meta-analyses involving many studies), audio or video clips, computer programs, and even primary or supplementary data sets. Of course, you should include these supplemental materials when you submit your report for peer review.

Editors and reviewers can assist you in determining what material is supplemental and what needs to be presented in the article proper. However, *supplemental materials* is a misleading label if it gives the impression that the information contained therein is less important than that found in the article. As the JARS suggests and I argue throughout this book, this information is not less important. In fact, the details of how research has been conducted and what it has found are essential to the advance of the social sciences. Some of these details are most vital to a more restricted audience—one that wants to know in detail what you did, why, and how they too might do the same thing—but the information is important nonetheless.

How This Book Can Help With Your Research

With this as background, in the chapters that follow I delve more deeply into the individual items called for in the JARS. As I discuss each item, I present a rationale for its inclusion. For some items, this is fairly obvious, whereas other items may require more explanation. For example, it is obvious why sugar is important in a chocolate cake, but exactly why does the recipe call for baking soda and baking powder rather than yeast? Then, I provide examples of good and not-so-good ways to present the information called for in the JARS. In Chapter 6, I present a companion set of standards also developed by the JARS Group for reporting meta-analyses, the MARS. In Chapter 7, I discuss in more detail the history of how JARS came to be as well as the potential use of JARS in the future. Finally, in the Appendix at the end of the book, I include the complete abstracts for all of the articles used as examples in the book.

If you are reading this book as you are writing a research report, the tables in the Appendix to this chapter not only provide a concise summary of the JARS but also can be easily photocopied and used as a checklist while you are working. It might also be good to have a copy of the *Publication Manual* (APA, 2010b) at hand because I refer to it frequently.

Appendix 1.1: Journal Article Reporting Standards (JARS)

Table A1.1. Journal Article Reporting Standards (JARS): Information Recommended for Inclusion in Manuscripts That Report New Data Collections Regardless of Research Design

Paper section and topic	Description

Title and title page	Identify variables and theoretical issues under investigation and the relationship between them
	Author note contains acknowledgment of special circumstances:
	  Use of data also appearing in previous publications, dissertations, or conference papers
	  Sources of funding or other support
	  Relationships that may be perceived as conflicts of interest

Abstract	Problem under investigation
	Participants or subjects; specifying pertinent characteristics; in animal research, include genus and species
	Study method, including:
	  Sample size
	  Any apparatus used
	  Outcome measures
	  Data-gathering procedures
	  Research design (e.g., experiment, observational study)
	Findings, including effect sizes and confidence intervals and/or statistical significance levels
	Conclusions and the implications or applications

Introduction	The importance of the problem:
	  Theoretical or practical implications
	Review of relevant scholarship:
	  Relation to previous work
	  If other aspects of this study have been reported on previously, how the current report differs from these earlier reports
	Specific hypotheses and objectives:
	  Theories or other means used to derive hypotheses
	  Primary and secondary hypotheses, other planned analyses
	How hypotheses and research design relate to one another

Method Participant characteristics	Eligibility and exclusion criteria, including any restrictions based on demographic characteristics Major demographic characteristics as well as important topic-specific characteristics (e.g., achievement level in studies of educational interventions), or in the case of animal research, genus and species

Sampling procedures	Procedures for selecting participants, including:
	  The sampling method if a systematic sampling plan was implemented
	  Percentage of sample approached that participated
	  Self-selection (either by individuals or units, such as schools or clinics)
	Settings and locations where data were collected
	Agreements and payments made to participants
	Institutional review board agreements, ethical standards met, safety monitoring

◼ **Table A1.1.** *(Continued)*

Paper section and topic	Description
Method (*continued*)	

Sample size, power, and precision	Intended sample size
	Actual sample size, if different from intended sample size
	How sample size was determined:
	    Power analysis, or methods used to determine precision of parameter estimates
	    Explanation of any interim analyses and stopping rules

Measures and covariates	Definitions of all primary and secondary measures and covariates:
	    Include measures collected but not included in this report
	Methods used to collect data
	Methods used to enhance the quality of measurements:
	    Training and reliability of data collectors
	    Use of multiple observations
	Information on validated or ad hoc instruments created for individual studies, for example, psychometric and biometric properties

Research design	Whether conditions were manipulated or naturally observed
	Type of research design; provided in Table A1.3 are modules for:
	    Randomized experiments (Module A1)
	    Quasi-experiments (Module A2)
	Other designs would have different reporting needs associated with them

Results	
Participant flow	Total number of participants Flow of participants through each stage of the study
Recruitment	Dates defining the periods of recruitment and repeated measurements or follow-up

Statistics and data analysis	Information concerning problems with statistical assumptions and/or data distributions that could affect the validity of findings
	Missing data:
	    Frequency or percentages of missing data
	    Empirical evidence and/or theoretical arguments for the causes of data that are missing, for example, missing completely at random (MCAR), missing at random (MAR), or missing not at random (MNAR)
	    Methods for addressing missing data, if used
	For each primary and secondary outcome and for each subgroup, a summary of:
	    Cases deleted from each analysis
	    Subgroup or cell sample sizes, cell means, standard deviations, or other estimates of precision, and other descriptive statistics
	    Effect sizes and confidence intervals
	For inferential statistics (null hypothesis significance testing), information about:
	    The a priori Type I error rate adopted
	    Direction, magnitude, degrees of freedom, and exact p level, even if no significant effect is reported
	For multivariable analytic systems (e.g., multivariate analyses of variance, regression analyses, structural equation modeling analyses, and hierarchical linear modeling) also include the associated variance–covariance (or correlation) matrix or matrices
	Estimation problems (e.g., failure to converge, bad solution spaces), anomalous data points
	Statistical software program, if specialized procedures were used
	Report any other analyses performed, including adjusted analyses, indicating those that were prespecified and those that were exploratory (though not necessarily in level of detail of primary analyses)

Ancillary analyses	Discussion of implications of ancillary analyses for statistical error rates

Discussion	Statement of support or nonsupport for all original hypotheses:
	    Distinguished by primary and secondary hypotheses
	    Post hoc explanations
	Similarities and differences between results and work of others
	Interpretation of the results, taking into account:
	    Sources of potential bias and other threats to internal validity
	    Imprecision of measures
	    The overall number of tests or overlap among tests
	    Other limitations or weaknesses of the study
	Generalizability (external validity) of the findings, taking into account:
	    The target population
	    Other contextual issues
	Discussion of implications for future research, program, or policy

Note. Adapted from "Reporting Standards for Research in Psychology: Why Do We Need Them? What Might They Be?" by APA Publications and Communications Board Working Group on Journal Article Reporting Standards, 2008, *American Psychologist, 63,* pp. 842–843. Copyright 2008 by the American Psychological Association.

Table A1.2. Module A: Reporting Standards for Studies With an Experimental Manipulation or Intervention (in Addition to Material Presented in Table A1.1)

Paper section and topic	Description
Method	
Experimental manipulations or interventions	Details of the interventions or experimental manipulations intended for each study condition, including control groups, and how and when manipulations or interventions were actually administered, specifically including:
	Content of the interventions or specific experimental manipulations
	Summary or paraphrasing of instructions, unless they are unusual or compose the experimental manipulation, in which case they may be presented verbatim
	Method of intervention or manipulation delivery
	Description of apparatus and materials used and their function in the experiment
	Specialized equipment by model and supplier
	Deliverer: who delivered the manipulations or interventions
	Level of professional training
	Level of training in specific interventions or manipulations
	Number of deliverers and, in the case of interventions, the *M*, *SD*, and range of number of individuals/units treated by each
	Setting: where the manipulations or interventions occurred
	Exposure quantity and duration: how many sessions, episodes, or events were intended to be delivered, how long they were intended to last
	Time span: how long it took to deliver the intervention or manipulation to each unit
	Activities to increase compliance or adherence (e.g., incentives)
	Use of language other than English and the translation method
Units of delivery and analysis	Unit of delivery: How participants were grouped during delivery
	Description of the smallest unit that was analyzed (and in the case of experiments, that was randomly assigned to conditions) to assess manipulation or intervention effects (e.g., individuals, work groups, classes)
	If the unit of analysis differed from the unit of delivery, description of the analytical method used to account for this (e.g., adjusting the standard error estimates by the design effect or using multilevel analysis)
Results	
Participant flow	Total number of groups (if intervention was administered at the group level) and the number of participants assigned to each group:
	Number of participants who did not complete the experiment or crossed over to other conditions, explain why
	Number of participants used in primary analyses
	Flow of participants through each stage of the study (see Figure A1.1)
Treatment fidelity	Evidence on whether the treatment was delivered as intended
Baseline data	Baseline demographic and clinical characteristics of each group
Statistics and data analysis	Whether the analysis was by intent-to-treat, complier average causal effect, other or multiple ways
Adverse events and side effects	All important adverse events or side effects in each intervention group
Discussion	Discussion of results taking into account the mechanism by which the manipulation or intervention was intended to work (causal pathways) or alternative mechanisms
	If an intervention is involved, discussion of the success of and barriers to implementing the intervention, fidelity of implementation
	Generalizability (external validity) of the findings, taking into account:
	The characteristics of the intervention
	How, what outcomes were measured
	Length of follow-up
	Incentives
	Compliance rates
	The "clinical or practical significance" of outcomes and the basis for these interpretations

Note. Adapted from "Reporting Standards for Research in Psychology: Why Do We Need Them? What Might They Be?" by APA Publications and Communications Board Working Group on Journal Article Reporting Standards, 2008, *American Psychologist, 63*, p. 844. Copyright 2008 by the American Psychological Association.

■ Table A1.3. Reporting Standards for Studies Using Random and Nonrandom Assignment of Participants to Experimental Groups

Paper section and topic	Description
Module A1: Studies using random assignment	
Method	
Random assignment method	Procedure used to generate the random assignment sequence, including details of any restriction (e.g., blocking, stratification)
Random assignment concealment	Whether sequence was concealed until interventions were assigned
Random assignment implementation	Who generated the assignment sequence
	Who enrolled participants
	Who assigned participants to groups
Masking	Whether participants, those administering the interventions, and those assessing the outcomes were unaware of condition assignments
	If masking took place, statement regarding how it was accomplished and how the success of masking was evaluated
Statistical methods	Statistical methods used to compare groups on primary outcome(s)
	Statistical methods used for additional analyses, such as subgroup analyses and adjusted analysis
	Statistical methods used for mediation analyses
Module A2: Studies using nonrandom assignment	
Method	
Assignment method	Unit of assignment (the unit being assigned to study conditions, e.g., individual, group, community)
	Method used to assign units to study conditions, including details of any restriction (e.g., blocking, stratification, minimization)
	Procedures employed to help minimize potential bias due to nonrandomization (e.g., matching, propensity score matching)
Masking	Whether participants, those administering the interventions, and those assessing the outcomes were unaware of condition assignments
	If masking took place, statement regarding how it was accomplished and how the success of masking was evaluated
Statistical methods	Statistical methods used to compare study groups on primary outcome(s), including complex methods for correlated data
	Statistical methods used for additional analyses, such as subgroup analyses and adjusted analysis (e.g., methods for modeling pretest differences and adjusting for them)
	Statistical methods used for mediation analyses

Note. Adapted from "Reporting Standards for Research in Psychology: Why Do We Need Them? What Might They Be?" by APA Publications and Communications Board Working Group on Journal Article Reporting Standards, 2008, *American Psychologist, 63,* p. 845. Copyright 2008 by the American Psychological Association.

■ **Figure A1.1.** Flow of Participants Through Each Stage of an Experiment or Quasi-Experiment

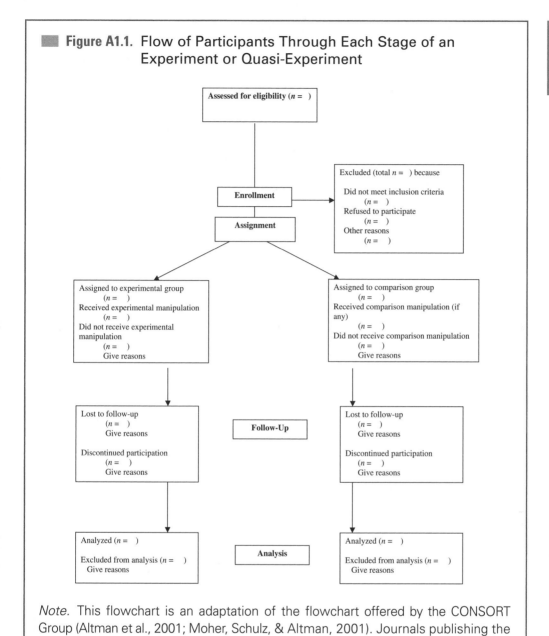

Note. This flowchart is an adaptation of the flowchart offered by the CONSORT Group (Altman et al., 2001; Moher, Schulz, & Altman, 2001). Journals publishing the original CONSORT flowchart have waived copyright protection.

Adapted from "Reporting Standards of Research in Psychology: Why Do We Need Them? What Might They Be?" by APA Publications and Communications Board Working Group on Journal Article Reporting Standards, 2008, *American Psychologist, 63*, p. 846. Copyright 2008 by the American Psychological Association.

2

Setting the Stage: The Title Page, Abstract, and Introduction

In this chapter, I examine the parts of a research report that set the stage for the description of how the study was carried out and what it found. The title and abstract alert potential readers to whether your study is related to the questions they need to have answered. The introduction section of the report places your work in a broader context and tells the reader why you think your work is important.

Title and Title Page

> Your title should identify the variables and theoretical issues under investigation and the relationship between them.

Shakespeare's Juliet pleaded that "a rose by any other name would smell as sweet" (*Romeo and Juliet,* Act 2, Scene 2, lines 43–44). What mattered most to her was not what something was called but rather its qualities. However, in the reporting of science, the name can matter greatly. The title given to a research report will help (or obscure) readers' understanding of the report's relevance to their needs.

When you conduct a computerized literature search using PsycINFO, for example, first you choose a search term or terms. Then, you specify the document fields—the parts of the document and document record—the computer should scan to find the terms. In PsycINFO, this list contains many different document fields. Depending on your reference database, the first listed field may be "All Text," but "Title" and "Abstract" are also listed as options. I suspect that these three fields are the most frequently used parameters for searches.

You might ask, "If my audience can search the full document, what difference does it make what terms are in the title?" The fact is that many, if not most, searchers will pass on the full document search. It will lead to the retrieval of too many documents that are not relevant to the question of interest, even if searchers use multiple keywords (and the "and" command) to narrow down the search. Wading through all of the document records that include a specified term or terms anywhere in the text can take lots of time better spent otherwise. If terms appear in titles and abstracts, they are more likely to be central to the document content.

Suppose you just wrote a report about a study in which you examined the effects of full-day kindergarten on children's academic achievement and psychological well-being. As you think about an appropriate title, you have a few things to consider. First, you would clearly want the terms *full-day kindergarten, academic achievement,* and *psychological well-being* in the title. However, what about specifying the comparison groups (e.g., half-day kindergarten, no kindergarten) against which full-day kindergarten's effects were compared? Further, psychological well-being is a broad construct. It might subsume other constructs, such as happiness, self-confidence, and optimism, and these might have been among the measures you used. You would want readers interested in these narrower constructs to find your report. Therefore, to be fully explanatory, the title might read

> Relative Effects of Full-Day Kindergarten Versus Half-Day and No Kindergarten on Children's Academic Achievement and Psychological Well-Being, Including Happiness, Self-Confidence, and Optimism

This title is about twice the length recommended (12 words) by the *Publication Manual* (American Psychological Association [APA], 2010b, p. 23), so a briefer title is called for, perhaps something like the following:

> Effects of Full-Day Kindergarten on Academic Achievement and Psychological Well-Being

Now your title is clear and concise but perhaps not precise. You might worry that searchers using the titles alone and looking for studies on children's happiness, self-concept, and/or optimism will miss your report. They will, but that is a trade-off you must make. However, you can minimize the chances your report will be missed by including these terms in the abstract. That way, searchers who use this broader level of document screening will find the report.

In picking the terms to include in your title, also consider what other terms might be used in the literature to refer to the same concept. For example, as you looked at the literature on the effects of full-day kindergarten, you might have discovered that some authors called it *all-day kindergarten.* It would be important to ensure that searchers using the term *all-day kindergarten* would retrieve your article. You should not put this alternative term in the title, but you can put it in the abstract, perhaps in parentheses after the first time *full-day kindergarten* is used. In constructing a title (and abstract), it is important to consider these other labels to ensure people who search on alternate terms for the same construct will find your report.

Authors are often tempted to think up catchy phrases to include in their titles. When searching was done by hand, this practice might have enticed readers to take a closer look at the article (and perhaps demonstrated how clever the author was). This practice has been diminishing in recent years. Authors may be discovering that extraneous elements in a clever title are a nuisance to them when they conduct computer searches. Now, they want to save others from similar bother; with rare exceptions, clever titles only add to the number of irrelevant documents retrieved. For example, suppose you titled an article

A Rose by Any Other Name Would Smell as Sweet: The Effects of Labels on Subjective Evaluations

The article would be retrieved by searches using the terms *rose, smell,* and *sweet,* terms unrelated to your article. Clever is okay if it communicates distinctive qualities of the study not captured elsewhere in the title, but be careful not to make the searcher's task more difficult by causing the retrieval of many irrelevant documents.[1]

Author Note

> Your author note should identify and describe special circumstances, for example,
>
> ■ use of data also appearing in previous publications, dissertations, and/or conference papers;
> ■ sources of funding or other support; and
> ■ relationships that may be perceived as conflicts of interest.

The title page of a manuscript should include an author note (APA, 2010b, pp. 24–25). The author note contains

■ the complete affiliations of the researchers at the time the study was conducted (first paragraph),
■ changes of affiliation if any author now works elsewhere (second paragraph),
■ acknowledgments of special circumstances and of people who assisted in conducting the study (through labor, expertise, etc.) but were not contributors in a way that led to authorship (third paragraph), and
■ information about how to contact the author who has taken responsibility for corresponding with readers who want more information (fourth paragraph).

The *Publication Manual* (APA, 2010b, pp. 18–19) and the *Ethical Principles of Psychologists and Code of Conduct (2002, Amended June 1, 2010),* hereinafter, the APA Ethics Code (APA, 2010a) provide guidance about who should get authorship credit and in what order. I have reproduced the relevant section from the APA Ethics Code in Exhibit 2.1.

When someone has contributed to the research but not at a level that warrants authorship, acknowledge this person in the author note. Typically, the acknowledgment

---

[1]Many authors begin their introduction with a quotation. This might be a good way to use your quotation from Ms. Capulet.

> ■ **Exhibit 2.1.**
>
> ## Excerpt From *Ethical Principles of Psychologists and Code of Conduct* Regarding Publication Credit
>
> ### 8.12 Publication Credit
>
> (a) Psychologists take responsibility and credit, including authorship credit, only for work they have actually performed or to which they have substantially contributed. (See also Standard 8.12b, Publication Credit.)
>
> (b) Principal authorship and other publication credits accurately reflect the relative scientific or professional contributions of the individuals involved, regardless of their relative status. Mere possession of an institutional position, such as department chair, does not justify authorship credit. Minor contributions to the research or to the writing for publications are acknowledged appropriately, such as in footnotes or in an introductory statement.
>
> (c) Except under exceptional circumstances, a student is listed as principal author on any multiple-authored article that is substantially based on the student's doctoral dissertation. Faculty advisors discuss publication credit with students as early as feasible and throughout the research and publication process as appropriate. (See also Standard 8.12b, Publication Credit.)
>
> *Note.* From *Ethical Principles of Psychologists and Code of Conduct* (2002, Amended June 1, 2010), p. 11, by the American Psychological Association, 2010, Washington, DC: Author. Copyright 2010 by the American Psychological Association.

begins with "We thank [person's name]," followed by a brief description of the nature of the contribution. For example, "We thank Joe Smith for comments on an earlier version of the manuscript" or "We thank Jane Johnson for assistance with statistical analyses."

Although all of these elements of an author note are essential, the Journal Article Reporting Standards (JARS) mentions only three special circumstances surrounding the data collection and its previous public appearances (contained in the third paragraph before the acknowledgment of others who contributed to the study). The first requires you to disclose the written, public venues through which the data or other unique ideas of your report have appeared previously. Thus, if the study served as all or part of your master's thesis or doctoral dissertation or if any written version of it is publically archived (e.g., a report to a funding agency), you need to say so in the author note. Such an acknowledgment might read, "This study served as Romeo Montague's doctoral dissertation at Capulet University." Typically, you do not have to report oral presentations of the study at meetings or conferences unless the conference presentations are eventually published.

The second special circumstance concerns acknowledging sources of support for the study other than the labor or expertise of an individual. If the study being reported was conducted with monetary or other forms of material support, acknowledge this in the author note. With regard to funding, some funding agencies require that they be acknowledged in this way; other funding agencies request that they not be acknowledged. Check with your funder before writing your author note. Also include the name of the person to whom the funds were awarded and the award number. This helps readers who want to follow up on the history of your work.[2] Your funder may also request a disclaimer indicating that the research does not reflect the views of the funding organization. The portion of the author note that acknowledges monetary support might read something like this:

> This research was supported by Grant 123456 from the Juliet Capulet Foundation to Romeo Montague. However, the research reported does not necessarily reflect the views of the Juliet Capulet Foundation.

Also, sometimes support comes in forms other than money. For example, a shopping mall might have permitted you to set up a table to collect data from shoppers, a community center might have provided a room for interviewing adolescents, or other researchers might have given you access to the stimulus materials or measures they used in a previous experiment. All of these in-kind contributions to the study should be acknowledged, with the consent of the provider, of course. Such an acknowledgment might read as follows:

> Thanks are extended to Capulet Florists for providing the roses used in this study.

Of course, you should be careful that the acknowledgment does not reveal anything that might compromise the confidentiality of the participants in your study.

The third, and equally critical, special circumstance concerns your need to acknowledge other publications in which some or all of the data you collected might have appeared. If you do not make this acknowledgment, you could be open to a charge of an ethical violation. The APA Ethics Code (APA, 2010a) states, "Psychologists do not publish, as original data, data that have been previously published. This does not preclude republishing data when they are accompanied by proper acknowledgment" (Standard 8.13, p. 11). For example, you should disclose in the author note if

- your study includes an analysis of longitudinal data and the first wave of data was published previously, or
- the data are part of a larger data set, portions of which were published previously.

This acknowledgment should be made whether or not the measures in your new report overlap with measures previously reported. The data still share many things in common with those in the original report.

Why is this important? The *Publication Manual* spells this out clearly (APA, 2010b, section 1.09, Duplicate and Piecemeal Publication of Data, pp. 13–15). Briefly, duplicate publication can (a) distort the scientific record by making a finding appear to have been replicated when this is not the case, (b) take up space that precludes the publication of other worthy reports, and/or (c) violate copyright laws. Read section 1.09 of the *Publication Manual* carefully. If your course of action is still not clear, contact the editor of the journal you want to submit to and ask for guidance.

Finally, in the author note you should disclose any possible conflicts of interest. Typically, a conflict of interest involves economic or commercial interests you or your

---

[2]In addition to serving as thanks to your funder, notes about your funding sources will help readers interested in your work who are looking for sources of support. Your grant history will help them see who is funding research related to their own.

coauthors have in the products or services used or discussed in the report. Again, the *Publication Manual* contains a discussion that will help you decide whether a potential conflict of interest exists (APA, 2010b, section 1.12, Conflict of Interest, pp. 17–18). Consult the *Publication Manual* as well as the editor if questions linger.

In the matters of both duplicate publication and conflict of interest, I suggest that you err on the side of caution: If you have any concern about either of these issues, say so in the author note when you first submit your article. When you submit your manuscript to APA, you will also be asked to verify on a form that you have complied with APA's ethical guidelines and disclosed any potential conflicts of interest. If your concern is immaterial, it is easier to remove this information later on than to explain its omission if it is later deemed important.

Abstract

Your abstract should provide a concise summary of the

- problem under investigation;
- participants or subjects, specifying pertinent characteristics (in animal research, include genus and species);
- study method, including sample size, any apparatus used, outcome measures, data-gathering procedures, and research design (e.g., experiment, observational study);
- findings, including effect sizes, confidence intervals, and/or statistical significance levels; and
- conclusions, implications, and/or applications.

The *Publication Manual* (APA, 2010b, section 2.04, pp. 25–27) points out that the abstract to your report "can be the most important single paragraph in an article" (p. 26). I have already noted that the abstract is important because for many researchers, its content will determine whether your article is retrieved in a computer-assisted literature search. Once retrieved, it is the first thing (perhaps the only thing) about your study that will be read. The *Publication Manual* says the abstract should be dense with information as well as accurate, nonevaluative (i.e., stick to the facts, no judgments), coherent, readable, and concise.

The elements of an abstract called for by the JARS are fairly self-explanatory. As examples of good abstracts, I have reproduced in Figure 2.1 two abstracts along with the other material, aside from the text, that appears on the first page of a published article for studies from two different areas of psychology. Note first that they both meet the length restrictions of the journals in which they appeared. These restrictions typically range from 150 to 250 words. Note also that the example abstract taken from Bricker et al. (2009) uses five bolded headings to highlight information about the study. The five headings correspond nicely to the information called for in the JARS. This type of abstract is called a *structured abstract,* and it is commonly found in the medical sciences. The editors of the journals that APA publishes are free to adopt this style

▓ Figure 2.1. Examples of Abstracts and Keywords in APA Journals

Health Psychology
2009, Vol.28, No.4, 439–447

© 2009 American Psychological Association
0278-6133/09/$12.00 DOI:10.1037/a0014568

Psychological and Social Risk Factors in Adolescent Smoking Transitions: A Population-Based Longitudinal Study

Jonathan B. Bricker, K. Bharat Rajan, Maureen Zalewski, M. Robyn Andersen,
Madelaine Ramey, and Arthur V. Peterson
Fred Hutchinson Cancer Research Center & University of Washington

Objective: This study longitudinally investigated psychological and social risk factors consistent with the theory of triadic influence (TTI) as predictors of adolescent smoking transitions. *Design:* Among 4,218 adolescents, 5 psychological risk factors (i.e., parent-noncompliance, friend-compliance, rebelliousness, low achievement motivation, and thrill seeking) were assessed in 9th grade (age14), 2 social influence risk factors (i.e., parents' and close friends' smoking) were assessed in Grades 3 (age 8) and 9 (age 14), respectively. *Main Outcome Measures:* Adolescent smoking transitions occurring between the 9th and 12th (ages 14–17) grade interval. *Results:* The probabilities contributed by each of the 5 psychological risk factors to the overall probability of making a specific smoking transition were as follows: 22% to 27% for the transition from never to trying smoking, 10% to 13% for the transition from trying to monthly smoking, and, for 3 of the 5 risk factors, 11% to 16% for the transition from monthly to daily smoking. For predicting trying smoking, the probability contributed by these psychological factors was greater than the probability contributed by each parent's and close friend's smoking. Parent-compliance had a higher contribution to the probability of trying smoking when an adolescent's parent smoked ($p < .05$), whereas friend-compliance had a higher contribution to the probability of trying smoking when an adolescent's friend smoked ($p < .001$). *Conclusion:* These psychological and social factors have an important influence on adolescent smoking transitions. Implications for TTI and smoking prevention interventions are discussed.

Keywords: psychological influences, parents, friends, adolescents, smoking

Neuropsychology
2009, Vol.23, No.5, 541–550

© 2009 American Psychological Association
0894-4105/09/$12.00 DOI:10.1037/a0016161

The Prevalence of Cortical Gray Matter Atrophy May Be Overestimated in the Healthy Aging Brain

Saartje Burgmans, Martin P. J. van Boxtel,
Eric F. P. M. Vuurman, Floortje Smeets,
and Ed H. B. M. Gronenschild
Maastricht University

Harry B. M. Uylings
Maastricht University and VU University
Medical Center Amsterdam

Jelle Jolles
Maastricht University and VU University Medical Center Amsterdam

Prevailing opinion holds that normal brain aging is characterized by substantial atrophy of cortical gray matter. However, this conclusion is based on earlier studies whose findings may be influenced by the inclusion of subjects with subclinical cognitive disorders like preclinical dementia. The present magnetic resonance imaging study tested this hypothesis. Cognitively healthy subjects (*M* age = 72 years, range = 52–82) who remained cognitively stable over a 3-year period were compared with subjects with significant cognitive decline. Subjects who developed dementia within 6 years after the scan session were excluded. The gray matter volumes of 7 cortical regions were delineated on T1-weighted magnetic resonance imaging scans. Participants without cognitive decline did not exhibit an age effect on the gray matter volume. Conversely, participants with cognitive decline exhibited a significant age effect in all the 7 areas. These results suggest that cortical gray matter atrophy may have been overestimated in studies on healthy aging because most studies were unable to exclude participants with a substantial atypical cognitive decline or preclinical dementia. Our results underscore the importance of establishing stringent inclusion criteria for future studies on normal aging.

Keywords: healthy aging, gray matter atrophy, cognitive decline, cerebral cortex, MRI

for articles on empirical studies, so it is not surprising, then, that you will see this structured format used frequently in journals like *Health Psychology*. Its purpose is to ensure that authors include the important information in the abstract.

Both example abstracts succinctly describe the problem under investigation. Burgmans et al. (2009) did so in three sentences, whereas Bricker et al. (2009) used just one. Then, each abstract introduces the principal design feature of the study and the important characteristics of the sample of participants. Bricker et al. did not actually mention that their study was a population-based longitudinal study, but this is clear from the title. Burgmans et al. mentioned the important apparatus they used for collecting data (magnetic resonance imaging), whereas Bricker et al. discussed the outcome variables collected by their measures. Each example abstract then presents the major findings. Bricker et al. presented some statistical results and probability levels associated with the findings (as called for in the JARS), whereas Burgmans et al. did not (their article did contain results of *t* tests and effect size estimates that might have been included).[3] Finally, each abstract concludes with a sentence or two that interpret the findings.

A final point: Both example abstracts are followed by keywords that can also be used to identify the report for a literature search. In fact, all authors publishing in APA journals are required to supply keywords for their articles. Note that some keywords in the examples are redundant with terms that appear in the title or abstract and others are not. Still other terms appear in the abstract that are not in the title or keywords that could very likely be the object of reference database searches. For Bricker et al. (2009), I suggest that *theory of triadic influence* and *achievement motivation;* for Burgmans et al. (2009), *dementia,* among others, would also be added as a keyword.

Introduction

Your introduction should include a

- statement of the problem under study and its importance;
- review of relevant scholarship, including its relation to previous work and, if other aspects of this study have been reported on previously, how the current study differs from these earlier studies;
- research strategy with
  - hypotheses and their derivation and rationale;
  - statement if hypotheses are primary or secondary; and
- statement regarding the relationship between hypotheses and research design.

The elements of the introduction section that are contained in the JARS correspond neatly with the text in the *Publication Manual* (APA, 2010b, section 2.05, pp. 27–28).

---

[3]Note as well that I have not updated the abstracts to meet the current requirements of APA Style as set forth in the *Publication Manual* (APA, 2010b) with regard to statistical significance. So, for example, Bricker et al.'s (2009) abstract reports two null hypothesis tests as $p < .05$ and $p < .001$. Under the new guidelines, these p levels would be reported precisely, using $p =$ rather than $p <$. At the time of the appearance of Bricker et al.'s article, what they did was perfectly acceptable.

The *Publication Manual* asks five questions that you need to answer at the beginning of your report:

- Why is this problem important?
- How does the study relate to previous work in the area?
- What are the primary and secondary hypotheses and objectives of the study? What, if any, are the links to theory?
- How do the hypotheses and research design relate to one another?
- What are the theoretical and practical implications of the study? (APA, 2010b, p. 27)

Here I focus only on the last two elements of the JARS: (a) stating whether hypotheses are primary or secondary and (b) describing the relationship between the hypotheses and the choice of research design.

Stating Whether Hypotheses Are of Primary or Secondary Interest

It is important to group hypotheses into those of primary interest and those of secondary interest to assist you and your readers in interpreting the results. This is especially critical with regard to the outcomes of statistical tests. For example, suppose you conducted a study concerning the effects of labels on people's evaluations of fragrances or perfumes. For a random half of participants, you labeled a fragrance (rated as *mildly pleasing* in previous tests) Roses, and for the other half, you labeled it Manure. After smelling the fragrance, you asked participants to rate it along, say, five dimensions (e.g., *pleasant–unpleasant*). Your primary hypothesis (contrary to Juliet's prediction that you would uncover a null finding) was that Roses would be rated as more pleasant than Manure. In addition, you asked participants questions about whether they would purchase the perfume, recommend it to a friend, and so on. For these measures, you are less confident you will find an effect of the label because you think the effect itself is not large and other considerations may obscure its impact. In the case of purchasing decisions, for example, people might already have a favorite fragrance. In your study, you also did some exploratory analyses by breaking your data down into subgroups and looking for interactions, for example, examining whether the labeling effect is greater for men or women. You have no strong predictions about what the outcome of the test might be. These hypotheses are secondary to your primary interest.

By dividing your hypotheses a priori into primary and secondary groups, you accomplish two things. First, suppose you had no a priori grouping. You ran a total of 20 tests pitting the null hypothesis against some alternative and found that three tests proved significant ($p = .05$). Given that we would expect one significant result even if all of your numbers were generated by chance, this is not a terribly impressive result.[4] (Juliet would be vindicated.) However, suppose all three significant findings were obtained on your five primary measures and all in the predicted direction. Now a more convincing argument for your hypothesis can be made.

Also, because the other 15 statistical tests have been labeled secondary, readers know to interpret these results in a different context. If the "intent to purchase" measure

---

[4]You may be familiar with the notion of experiment-wise error rates. This refers to the fact that because you have conducted more than one statistical comparison, the probability that you will get at least one false rejection of the null hypothesis is greater than the probability associated with each individual comparison. The more tests you do, the more likely an experiment-wise error will occur.

does not prove significant, readers know that a priori you viewed this test as less diagnostic of your main hypothesis. Conversely, if you find men and women do differ in the effect of the label, you will have to provide a post hoc explanation for why one sex was more affected than the other. This after-the-fact hypothesis will need further testing before it gains the credibility that your study bestowed on your primary hypotheses. In this way, an a priori grouping of hypotheses helps both you and your audience interpret your results.[5]

Stating the Relationship Between Your Hypotheses and Research Design

It is also important in the introduction section to briefly explain your research design and why the design is well suited to answer your research question. So, for example, if your research question addresses a causal relationship (e.g., does the label of a fragrance cause people to react to it differently?), an experimental or quasi-experimental research design is appropriate for answering it. If the question relates to a simple association (are labels for fragrances that are rated more positively associated with more positive reactions to the fragrance itself?), then a simple correlational analysis may provide the answer. If you are interested in how people differ, then a between-subjects design is called for. If your interest is in how people change over time, then a within-subjects design is most appropriate.

The JARS recommends that you provide your audience with an analysis of the fit between your research question and research design in the introduction section of your article. Why did you pick this design to answer this question? How well can this design answer the question? This will be critical to readers' evaluation of your article. If you ask a causal question but your design does not support a causal interpretation, you have made a mistake. By setting this out explicitly in the introduction section, you will be less likely to make an inferential error, and your readers will be less likely to misinterpret your results. On occasion, your intentions (the design you hoped to carry out) will be thwarted by the realities you faced in conducting the study. In the end, your hoped-for inferences and design will not match up. In such cases, you need to describe these problems in the Method section (which I turn to in Chapter 3) and address their implications in the Discussion section.

---

[5]Another way to address the issue of experiment-wise error would be to combine your related measures, perhaps through factor analysis, so that you did fewer tests. The optimal strategy to address experiment-wise error may be to do both: Combine related measures and group the combined measures on the basis of their primary or secondary status.

Detailing What You Did: The Method Section

3

The Method section of your article is the place where you describe how you carried out your study. The information shared here should include who participated, what you did, and what instruments you used. Cast broadly, these are the most important questions to answer as you write your Method section:

■ What information will readers need to evaluate the validity of your study's conclusions and to interpret its findings?

■ What information would readers need to know if they wished to replicate your research?

Both of these questions need to be answered in full for your article and your research to be of maximum use to others.

Answering the first question completely will almost certainly cause you some anxiety. Because the perfect study has yet to be conducted, you will find yourself in the uncomfortable situation of having to reveal the flaws in your work. Should you report the number of participants who chose not to take part in the study after it was explained to them? Should you describe the measure you collected that proved unreliable or was misunderstood by many participants and therefore went unanalyzed? The answer is "Yes, report the flaws."

Answering the second question requires you to think about those things you did that were critical to getting your results. Replication is central to science. It is always in your interest to provide enough detail, the good and the bad, so that someone else can verify what you found by redoing your study.

When it comes to writing about the methods of your study, the Journal Article Reporting Standards (JARS) can be thought of as an attempt to systematize aspects of research methodology known to have a significant influence on how a study is interpreted and what is needed to replicate it. The JARS items take some of the guesswork out of reporting the methods of your research. They also are meant to protect you against accusations that you purposely did not report things. Again, however, for any particular study in any particular subfield of psychology, there will be unique features that render some of the JARS items irrelevant whereas other important items may need them to be included in your report. Because of this, I draw on 14 articles across a wide range of topics to present examples of the different items on the JARS. I skip around from article to article, so I remind you of the important characteristics of each study as it is reintroduced. If you get lost, the Appendix at the end of this book provides the abstract for each of the 14 articles in alphabetical order by author. You can refer to these to keep on track.

Characteristics of Participants and the Sampling Procedures

Your description of participant characteristics should include

- eligibility and exclusion criteria, including any restrictions based on demographic characteristics, and
- major demographic characteristics as well as important topic-specific characteristics (e.g., achievement level in studies of educational interventions) or, in the case of animal research, genus and species.

Your description of the sampling procedures should include

- the sampling method if a systematic sampling plan was implemented;
- the percentage of sample approached that participated;
- self-selection (by either individuals or units, such as schools or clinics);
- settings and locations where data were collected;
- agreements and payments made to participants; and
- institutional review board agreements, ethical standards met, and safety monitoring.

Most Method sections begin with a description of who took part in the study and how they were recruited. Some people will always be more likely than others to participate in a study, often simply because some people are convenient to recruit. For example, your hypothetical perfume labeling study, like many studies in psychology, may have been conducted with undergraduates drawn from the subject pool of your psychology department who may have participated as part of a course's requirements. Such samples are restricted primarily to young adults going to college in a particular part of a country who have at least a curiosity about psychology. Studies drawing participants from communities that are near an institution of higher learning are also restricted in some ways, at least geographically. Even samples meant to be nationally representative can include restrictions based on, for example, language and/or accessibility.

It is important to identify and report the ways in which your recruitment procedure might have restricted the types of people in your study. Restrictions on who participated may influence the interpretation of your data. Readers will ask, "Whom do the results of this study apply to?" and you will address this question explicitly in your Discussion section. More specifically, you and your readers will ask the following questions:

- What is the target population to which the issue under study pertains?
- Are the people in the study drawn from this population?

If the answer to the second question is "no," then your study may not be relevant to the pertinent issue. If the answer is "yes," then a third question would be

- Are the people in the study in some way a restricted subsample of the target population?

If they are,

- Do the restrictions suggest that the results pertain to some, but not all, members of the target population?

This last question rules the day. Drawing a random sample from your target population (a sample in which each population element had an equal chance of being picked) is ideal. However, researchers know this is rarely feasible. Given this, what becomes most important is that either (a) the ways your sample differs from the target population are irrelevant to drawing inferences about the population of interest or (b) you are careful (in your Discussion section) to point out how the restrictions on your sample might limit your ability to draw inferences about certain subpopulations within the target population.

To continue with the example of the perfume labeling study, what was the population of interest? Presumably it was all humans, unless, perhaps, it was a marketing study aimed at women in the United States. Are undergraduates drawn from this population? Yes. Are undergraduates a restricted subsample of all humans or all U.S. women? Yes, but does it matter? To answer this extrastatistical question about your data and inferences, readers (and you) need to know as precisely as possible what the characteristics of your sample were and how participants were recruited.

Let's look at some examples of how participant characteristics and sampling procedures are described in published research articles. Goldinger, He, and Papesh (2009) reported a study in their article "Deficits in Cross-Race Face Learning: Insights From Eye Movements and Pupillometry," which was published in the *Journal of Experimental Psychology: Learning, Memory, and Cognition*. They examined the *own-race bias*, a phenomenon in which people are better at recognizing and discriminating faces from their own race than those from other races. They conducted two experiments, one with Caucasian participants and one with Asian participants. Here is how Goldinger et al. described the participants in their first study:

> *Participants.* The initial sample included 46 Arizona State University students, all volunteers who received course credit. All participants reported either normal or corrected vision. From the original sample, data were excluded from six students. Two were Asian, three had excessive periods of eye-tracking failure, and one failed to complete the recognition test. The final sample included 40 students, with 20 per study-time condition. All were Caucasian and reported no special familiarity with Asian faces. (p. 1107)

Even though this description is brief, Goldinger et al. (2009) did a good job of addressing the issues regarding participant characteristics and sampling procedures called for by the JARS. They made it clear that the participants were in Arizona (location), that they were drawn from a college subject pool (setting), and that they received course credit for participating (agreements and payments). In this first of two studies, an eligibility criterion was that participants had to be Caucasian (in the second study, they had to be Asian) and have no special familiarity with Asian faces (what this might be is not defined). Participants had to have normal or corrected vision.

As a critical reader or potential replicator of this study, do you have the information you need? It is hard to see much missing. For example, you are not told the sex composition of the sample, but does this matter? Probably not; at this time, theories about the own-race bias suggest no reason to believe that the phenomenon operates differently for male and female participants.[1] Note as well that Goldinger et al. (2009) reported that four participants were eliminated for procedural reasons, eye-tracking failures, and incomplete data. This is a small portion of the otherwise eligible initial sample, probably not large enough to concern us. What if eight or 18 participants had to be dropped from the experiment? Then you might consider whether the exclusion criteria are related to own-race bias. To push a point, only college students were participants. If you want to draw inferences about all humans, could it be that college students are less (or more) susceptible to the own-race bias than younger or older humans with more or less education? These are issues that might interest you. From the JARS point of view, however, the authors have given us what we need to consider these issues.

Next is a more complex description of a sampling procedure and the resulting participants' characteristics. It is from Fagan, Palkovitz, Roy, and Farrie's (2009) article "Pathways to Paternal Engagement: Longitudinal Effects of Risk and Resilience on Non-resident Fathers," published in *Developmental Psychology*. The researchers wanted to know whether risk factors (e.g., fathers' drug problems, incarceration, unemployment) were associated with resilience factors (e.g., fathers' positive attitudes, job training, religious participation) and paternal engagement with offspring. Here is how Fagan et al. described their sampling procedure and participant characteristics:

> The FFCW [Fragile Families and Child Wellbeing Study] follows a cohort of nearly 5,000 children born in the United States between 1998 and 2000 (McLanahan & Garfinkel, 2000). The study oversamples births to unmarried couples, and when weighted, the data are representative of nonmarital births in large U.S. cities at the turn of the century. . . . The sample is made up of 3,712 unwed couples and 1,186 married couples.
>
> The present study made use of the birth (baseline), 1-year follow-up (Year 1), and 3-year follow-up (Year 3) fathers' and mothers' data. Our sample was selected in several steps. First, we selected fathers who participated at baseline and who were not married and were not residing with the mother most or all of the time. . . . We excluded married and cohabiting couples at baseline to ensure that the study focused on the most fragile families at the time of the child's birth.

---

[1]At some later date, if the sex of the perceiver does come to be seen as a potential moderator of own-race bias, future replicators may wish they had this information (and meta-analysts would be frustrated over it not being given), but Goldinger et al. (2009) cannot be faulted for this lack of prescience. That said, to the extent that you can foresee and describe the characteristics of participants in your studies that might prove critical in the future, the greater will be the long-term value of your study.

Next, we selected fathers who also participated at Year 1. Of the 815 eligible fathers who participated at baseline and Year 1, 130 were missing substantial data, so we removed them from the sample. These steps resulted in a sample of 685 fathers. We then excluded fathers who were not interviewed at Year 3, yielding a sample of 569 fathers. About 4% of the 569 fathers had substantial missing Year 3 data that could not be easily imputed. We omitted these fathers from the study, yielding a final sample of 549 fathers with complete data. . . .

Participants

The average age of the fathers in the sample was about 26 years at the baseline interview. . . . The majority of fathers were African American (72.3%), followed by Hispanic (16.2%) and White (9.5%). Nearly 40% of the fathers completed less than high school or less than a general equivalency diploma. Shifts in father–mother relational quality occurred across time. One year after the child's birth, most fathers were in romantic relationships (51.9%) with the mother, 6.4% were married, 28.4% were friends, 13.2% were acquaintances, and one father was separated from the mother. By the 3rd-year follow-up, 9% of fathers were married, 36% were in romantic relationships with the mother, 35% were friends, and 15.5% described the mother of the baby as an acquaintance. Substantial proportions of fathers resided with their child at Year 1 (37.7%) and Year 3 (41.2%). (pp. 1392–1393)

Fagan et al. (2009) made the case that the sample used in their study was initially drawn from a wide geographical space and with the intent of its being representative of nonmarital births in the United States. They also carefully filled in readers about a series of exclusion criteria they applied to the initial sample. Some of the exclusion criteria relate to identifying the subpopulation of interest to them, and some, regrettably, relate to their inability to obtain complete data from participants in the broader study, families that would have been included had data been complete.

Let me highlight two aspects of the description. First, Fagan et al. (2009) made it clear that they were using a data set that has been used to study other questions related to fragile families and child well-being. They told readers where to obtain more information about the larger sample (McLanahan & Garfinkel, 2000). Thus, as detailed as Fagan et al.'s description is, it still does not answer all of the JARS questions. Not to worry. McLanahan and Garfinkel (2000), in their working paper, did this for you.[2] In fact, nearly all of the working paper is a detailed description of the instruments, sampling procedures, and characteristics of the sample. It would have been a poor use of journal space for Fagan et al. to reproduce all of this material when the original report is easily available on the Internet. Instead, they focused on how they resampled from the initial sample and the resulting characteristics of their subsample.

Second, note that the description of the final sample used in the study is very detailed. McLanahan and Garfinkel (2000) even provided a table (reproduced here as Table 3.1)

---

[2]McLanahan and Garfinkel (2000) stated that "the sample is representative of nonmarital births in each [sampled] city and is nationally representative of nonmarital births to parents residing in cities with populations over 200,000" (pp. 14–16).

Table 3.1. Example of Table Reporting Demographic Characteristics of a Sample

Demographic Characteristics of Sample

Variable	Baseline	Year 1	Year 3
Father's age, *M* (*SD*)	26 (7.4)		
Father's race/ethnicity, *n* (%)			
White	52 (9.5)		
African American	397 (72.3)		
Hispanic	89 (16.2)		
Other	11 (2.0)		
Father's education, *n* (%)			
Less than high school diploma	213 (38.8)		
High school diploma	146 (26.6)		
General equivalency diploma	55 (10.0)		
Some college	95 (17.3)		
Technical training	19 (3.5)		
College graduate	13 (2.4)		
Graduate school	8 (1.5)		
Father–mother relationship, *n* (%)			
Romantic	436 (79.4)	285 (51.9)	198 (36.1)
Friends	71 (12.9)	156 (24.5)	192 (35.0)
Acquaintances	42 (7.7)	72 (13.2)	85 (15.5)
Married		35 (6.4)	51 (9.3)
Separated		1 (0.2)	23 (4.2)
Father resides with child, *n* (%)		207 (37.7)	226 (41.2)
Child's gender, *n* (%)			
Male	276 (50.3)		
Female	273 (49.7)		
Father has other biological children, *n* (%)	280 (51.0)		

Note. Adapted from "Pathways to Paternal Engagement: Longitudinal Effects of Risk and Resilience on Nonresident Fathers," by J. Fagan, R. Palkovitz, K. Roy, and D. Farrie, 2009, *Developmental Psychology, 45,* p. 1393. Copyright 2009 by the American Psychological Association.

with information more specific than that included in the text. This will make it much easier for future researchers who attempt to replicate the finding to compare their sample with that used by Fagan et al. (2009). The description is an excellent example of how to report sampling procedures and participant characteristics when samples are drawn to be broadly representative. It meets the JARS standards. As a critical reader, between this document and the earlier working paper, you have all you need to determine who the target population was, how the sample in the study might differ from the target population, and whether you think the differences matter. As a potential replicator, you would not have to ask for more information.

Neither Goldinger et al. (2009) nor Fagan et al. (2009) explicitly stated that they received permission from an institutional review board to run their study or that they followed ethical standards in doing so. Requiring such a statement is a relatively new practice and one that should be followed in the future. In your study of labeling effects, you might write, "The Capulet University Institutional Review Board gave approval for the research." Sometimes you will see a statement of this type in the author note rather than the Method section.

Finally, it is important to point out that although the characteristics of settings and participants are very different, researchers who work with animals are under the same obligations to provide detailed descriptions of subjects. Here, for example, is a description of the animals used in a study by Killeen, Sanabria, and Dolgov (2009) from an article titled "The Dynamics of Conditioning and Extinction" that was published in the *Journal of Experimental Psychology: Animal Behavior Processes:*

Subjects

Six experienced adult homing pigeons (*Columba livia*) were housed in a room with a 12-hr light–dark cycle, with lights on at 6:00 a.m. They had free access to water and grit in their home cages. Running weights were maintained just above their 80% ad libitum weight; a pigeon was excluded from a session if its weight exceeded its running weight by more than 7%. When required, supplementary feeding of Ace-Hi pigeon pellets (Star Milling Co., Perris, CA) was given at the end of each day, no fewer than 12 hr before experimental sessions were conducted. Supplementary feeding amounts were based equally on current deviation and on a moving average of supplements over the past 15 sessions. (p. 449)

Clearly, not only the type of pigeon but also the pigeons' weights were important considerations in this study. In some areas of animal research, researchers are expected to report the genus, species, and strain number or other characteristics needed to identify animals, such as the name and location of the supplier and the stock designation. Sometimes, researchers are expected to report the animals' sex, age, and other physiological conditions. The reasoning that you must apply in deciding what to report about animals in a study is no different than the reasoning applied when deciding what to report for people. As the *Publication Manual* stated, "Appropriate identification of research participants is critical to the science and practice of psychology, particularly for generalizing the findings, making comparisons across replications, and using the evidence in research syntheses and secondary data analyses" (APA, 2010b, p. 29).

Sample Size, Power, and Precision

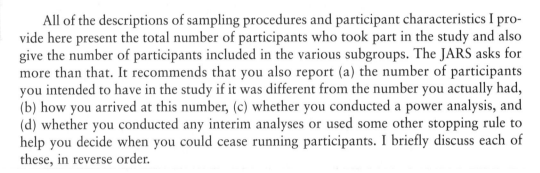

When describing the size, power, and precision of your sample, include

- intended sample size;
- actual sample size, if different from intended sample size; and
- how sample size was determined by
  - power analysis or methods used to determine precision of parameter estimates and
  - explanation of any interim analyses and stopping rules.

All of the descriptions of sampling procedures and participant characteristics I provide here present the total number of participants who took part in the study and also give the number of participants included in the various subgroups. The JARS asks for more than that. It recommends that you also report (a) the number of participants you intended to have in the study if it was different from the number you actually had, (b) how you arrived at this number, (c) whether you conducted a power analysis, and (d) whether you conducted any interim analyses or used some other stopping rule to help you decide when you could cease running participants. I briefly discuss each of these, in reverse order.

Stopping Rules

Stopping rules refer to predetermined criteria for deciding what statistical results you would find adequate to stop collecting data from additional participants. Typically, this relates to the acceptable Type I error rate you have selected or the chance that you falsely rejected a true null hypothesis. For example, you might decide that you will run participants in your labeling study until your statistical test of the difference between the two groups (the roses and manure groups) rejects the null hypothesis of no difference at the $p = .05$ level of significance. Then you check your significance level frequently after collecting data from new participants and end the experiment when the designated p level is reached.

The use of stopping rules is rare in most areas of psychology; there is some possibility that the researchers will capitalize on chance. That is, because of a run of "good luck" in participant data, the difference between groups on the primary dependent variables in the observed sample might be larger than the true difference in the population. If more participants took part in the study, the observed difference could return to a smaller estimated value closer to the population difference.[3] Stopping rules are

---

[3]As an example, a study of treatments for leukemia initially showed unusually large effects but the evaluation was continued anyway. With more data, the effects disappeared. This led Wheatley and Clayton (2003) to suggest, "Lessons to be learned from this example are that: fixed stopping rules based on some predetermined p-value should not be used and the decision to close a randomization or not should take account of other factors such as the medical plausibility of the magnitude of the treatment effect; chance effects do occur and happen more frequently than many clinicians realize" (p. 66). It is also the case that stopping rules can be used to halt experiments in which the treatment appears to be ineffective (Lachin, 2005).

used most often in medical research and some psychology research related to health and medicine (but not in labeling studies). Their use is most likely to occur when researchers are evaluating a critical treatment, for example, the effectiveness of a cancer drug; there are ethical concerns raised by not stopping the research when lives may be lost by withholding the treatment while further evidence is collected.[4]

Interim Analysis

An interim analysis looks a lot like a stopping rule, but here the decisions are more post hoc. You might decide that you will collect data from 15 participants in each of your labeling conditions and then look at the data to determine whether your results have reached statistical significance. If they have, your study might be over. If not, you might calculate the effect size in the collected data and use this to conduct a power analysis. The result of this power analysis is then used to decide how many more participants to test. A brief treatment of ethical and statistical issues related to stopping rules and interim analyses in medicine is provided by Pocock (2007).

Effect Size

It is important to define two terms I just introduced: *effect size* and *power analysis*. Cohen (1988) has defined an effect size as "the degree to which the phenomenon is present in the population, or the degree to which the null hypothesis is false" (pp. 9–10). Although numerous metrics for expressing effect sizes are available, three metrics are used most often in the literature.

The first is called the *standardized mean difference*, or d index. This is the metric you would use in your labeling study. The d index is a scale-free measure of the separation between two group means. Continuing the labeling study example, calculating the d index involves dividing the difference between the roses and manure group means by their average standard deviation.[5] So, if $d = 0.50$, it means half of a standard deviation separates the two group means.

Another effect-size metric is the r index, or the Pearson product–moment correlation coefficient. (You may be familiar with this effect size.) Typically, it is used to measure the linear relation between two continuous variables. You would use this measure if you studied, for example, the relationship between people's affective ratings of the names of perfumes currently on the market and their reactions to the fragrance itself.

The third effect-size metric is the odds ratio. It is used when both variables are dichotomous, and findings are presented as frequencies or proportions. You might use an odds ratio (or a number of related metrics) to express the strength of the relationship between your two labels and whether participants said they would buy the fragrance. To calculate an odds ratio, you would determine the odds of purchasing in each condition, say 6 to 1 in the manure condition and 3 to 1 in the roses condition. The odds ratio in this situation is 2, meaning the odds of purchasing the fragrance are twice as great when it is called Roses than when called Manure.

---

[4]Stopping rules are also used in other statistical contexts, for example, in stepwise regression (for deciding how many variables to add to or remove from a model) and factor analysis (for deciding how many factors to retain).
[5]There are finer nuances to the calculation of d indexes that I do not go into here (see Grissom & Kim, 2005).

How do you know what effect size to expect in your study? This is where the interim analysis comes in: Use it to estimate your expected effect size. Or, you can look at the effect sizes that have been found in previous studies on the same topic when similar methods have been used (meta-analyses are especially good for this purpose; they always include effect size estimates). Another option would be to decide what effect size would be theoretically or practically meaningful, for example, how large a sales difference would matter in a perfume company's decision about what to call a perfume.

Power Analysis

A power analysis most often is used to determine how many participants should be included in a study to have a good chance of rejecting the null hypothesis. Here, when you conduct a power analysis, you decide a priori (a) what you expect the effect size to be (or what effect size will be meaningful),[6] (b) what p level you will use to reject the null hypothesis, and (c) the likelihood with which you want to be able to reject the null hypothesis if there truly is a relationship in the population. This last number is referred to as the *power* of your study. If power equals .80, it means you have an 80% chance of rejecting the null hypothesis given your chosen statistical significance level, sample size, and expected effect size.[7] Say you expect an effect size of $d = 0.50$, and you want an 80% chance of rejecting the null hypothesis at $p = .05$ (two-tailed). With these three numbers, you can then calculate power or, more likely, you will consult a power table (see Cohen, 1988). You will discover that you need to include 64 participants per condition to have 80% power.

Here is an example of how a power analysis should be reported. It is taken from Amir et al.'s (2009) article titled "Attention Training in Individuals With Generalized Social Phobia: A Randomized Controlled Trial" that was published in the *Journal of Consulting and Clinical Psychology*. The researchers reported an experimental study on generalized anxiety disorder (GAD) that examined the effectiveness of an attention modification training procedure in which individuals were trained to divert their attention from a threatening social stimulus:

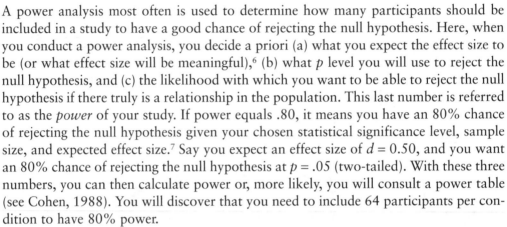

> On the basis of prior research examining the effect of a similar eight-session attention bias modification procedure on symptoms of anxiety in a sample of individuals diagnosed with GAD (Amir et al., 2009), we estimated an average effect size of [$d =$] 1.0 on our primary dependent measures. With alpha set at .05 and power (1-beta) set at .80, a sample size of at least 17 participants per group was needed to detect an effect of this magnitude between the AMP [attention modification program] and ACC [attention control condition] groups on the primary outcome measures of social anxiety symptoms. (Amir et al., 2009, p. 966)

Amir et al. included 22 participants in one condition and 26 in the other.

---

[6]Again, this can be determined by what was found in past research or by theoretical or practical importance. Still, it is important to keep in mind that in addition to setting your tolerance for making false positive conclusions and for missing true positive conclusions, the power of your study will depend on your expectations about (estimated impact of) the very thing you are trying to determine.

[7]Sometimes power analyses are conducted after a study has been run and has failed to reject the null hypothesis. Here the researchers may be hoping to make the case that the study was underpowered for revealing a significant result (i.e., the sample was too small or the effect too subtle).

Intended Sample Size

It is rare to find explicit statements of the sample size that researchers intended to include in their studies. It is more often the case that you can discern this from other information. Amir et al. (2009) made it clear that a minimum sample size was 17 per condition, and they surpassed this figure. In other instances, the researchers provide the total number of people in the population or subpopulation of interest, and this can be taken as an indication of the intended sample size. For example, O'Neill, Vandenberg, DeJoy, and Wilson (2009) reported a study titled "Exploring Relationships Among Anger, Perceived Organizational Support, and Workplace Outcomes" in the *Journal of Occupational Health Psychology*. They examined the relationships between perceived organizational support; employee anger; and turnover, absences, and accidents on the job:

> Respondents were 1,136 employees from 21 stores of a national retail organization headquartered in the southeastern United States. There were a total of 4,274 employees across the 21 locations; 1,495 people (35%) completed the survey and, of those, 76% provided usable responses for purposes of this study. . . . In summary, 27% of all employees in the 21 locations provided usable data. The average number of respondents per store was 71, with a range of 36 to 138. (O'Neill et al., 2009, p. 323)

Clearly, the intended sample was all of the employees ($N = 4,274$) in the 21 locations.

If you are conducting a study that involves the comparison of people in different conditions, the best way to ensure that you have provided complete information about your sample size is to use the flowchart in Figure A1.1. This guides you through each of the steps involved in the sampling process and helps you document when and why participants were lost from your study. Figure A1.1 can help you and your readers determine both the legitimate generalizations (about people) that can be made from your study and whether your study had sufficient power to reject the null hypothesis or, in effect size terms, whether your study could estimate the effect sizes with sufficient precision. I provide examples of the use of Figure A1.1 when I discuss the Results section.

Measures

> Your description of the measures and covariates should include
>
> - definitions of all primary and secondary measures and covariates, including measures collected but not included in this report;
> - methods used to collect data;
> - methods used to enhance the quality of measurements, including training and reliability of data collectors and use of multiple observations; and
> - information on validated or ad hoc instruments created for individual studies, for example, psychometric and biometric properties.

The JARS also recommends that your Method section include a subsection that provides definitions of all measures you collected on participants. Definitions of measures should be provided regardless of whether these were outcome variables of primary or secondary interest to you or whether you used them as covariates in your analyses of outcome variables. Also, you should describe measures that you collected but did not use in the reported analyses. These unanalyzed measures can be mentioned briefly, sometimes in a footnote. Or, if they are described in another document that is publicly available—such as an already-published journal article based on the same data collection, a dissertation, or a technical report—you can simply include a reference for this work.

This subsection should also describe the methods used to collect the measures. Did you use written questionnaires, interviews, or behavior assessments or observations? Also, report any techniques you used to improve the quality of the measurements, such as training observers or using multiple observations. Finally, report information on the validity and reliability of your measures or their biometric properties, if this is available.

I discussed in Chapter 2 of this volume (pp. 21–22) the distinction between primary and secondary measures, so I do not repeat that information here. Covariates are variables that may be predictive of the outcome variable in your study. You enter them into your data analysis to either (a) reduce the error in the outcome measure to make your statistical tests more sensitive to the effects of other variables or (b) adjust for initial differences between experimental groups (on the covariate and therefore possibly on the outcome measure) because participants were not randomly assigned to conditions (or randomization failed).

An example of a measurement description that meets the JARS recommendations comes from a study by Tsaousides et al. (2009), in the article "The Relationship Between Employment-Related Self-Efficacy and Quality of Life Following Traumatic Brain Injury," published in *Rehabilitation Psychology:*

Predictor Variables

Employment-related self-efficacy. The Perceived Employability subscale (PEM) of the Bigelow Quality of Life Questionnaire (BQQ; Bigelow, McFarland, Gareau, & Young, 1991) was used to measure employment-related self-efficacy. The PEM consists of eight items that assess an individual's confidence to find and maintain employment (e.g., how comfortable do you feel going out to look for a job?). Items are rated on a 4-point Likert scale and summed, with higher scores indicating higher efficacy. Only five of the eight items from the PEM subscale were included . . . with adequate internal consistency (Cronbach's $\alpha = .72$). (p. 301)

This description reveals the construct of interest (employment-related self-efficacy), how it was measured (with a questionnaire), that the measure had five questions each with four possible responses, and that the internal consistency of the measure was adequate. Here, Tsaousides et al. (2009) provided Cronbach's alpha, which uses the correlations between items to estimate internal consistency. Many other measures of internal consistency exist (Kline, 2005). Tsaousides et al. also provided an example of a question on the questionnaire. This is good practice, especially when the content of questions is not clear or when the measure involves multiple items that are summed to derive a participant's score. It is best practice to provide a reference to a document that spells out the entire measure and its measurement characteristics or a link (along with your example) to an online supplemental archive, where you provide the reader with the complete measurement instrument.

Here is a good description of a measurement scale based on observer ratings. Rather than a measure of behavior, this scale measures the quality of preschool classrooms. It is taken from Moller, Forbes-Jones, and Hightower's (2008) article "Classroom Age Composition and Developmental Change in 70 Urban Preschool Classrooms," published in the *Journal of Educational Psychology*:

> **Early Childhood Environment Rating Scale—Revised (ECERS–R).** The ECERS–R is among the most widely used observational tools allowing for objective assessment of preschool classroom quality (Henry et al., 2004; Howes & Smith, 1995; Scarr, Eisenberg, & Deater-Deckard, 1994). The seven areas of classroom quality that the ECERS–R measures are space and furnishing, personal care routines, language and reasoning, activities, interaction, program structure, and parents and staff. Each area contains five to 10 items that represent various elements of that area. For the present investigation, we averaged scores across all seven areas to create an overall, composite measure of classroom quality. . . .
>
> ECERS–R observations of classroom quality were conducted by 24 observers midway through the academic year (in the months of February, March, and April). For classroom observers in their 1st year of training, ECERS–R observers attended a 15-hr training program and reached an interrater reliability of 85% agreement with a master observer who was trained by the ECERS–R authors. For observers in their 2nd year, an additional 4–5 hr of training were required. All observers maintained an interrater reliability of 80% agreement, with 20% of their observations being checked. (pp. 744–745)

Moller et al. gave several references in which readers can find additional information on the measurement. Because this measure involves observations, the authors were careful to describe how raters were trained and how reliable their ratings were. Moller et al. provided an agreement percentage as a measure of interrater reliability. Other measures of rater equivalence could also have been reported (Kline, 2005).

Finally, biometric properties refer to the characteristics of individuals' physical or physiological makeup. Some biometric properties, such as age, are easy to collect with great reliability. Others require descriptions with much detail. For example, an electrocardiogram (EKG) obtained by strategically placing electrodes on the skin of participants is a measure of the heart's electrical activity. In Taylor and James's (2009) article "Evidence for a Putative Biomarker for Substance Dependence," published in *Psychology of Addictive Behaviors*, the authors used an EKG as one measure in a study examining differences in responses to predictable and unpredictable bursts of white noise by people with and without substance dependence. Here is their description of how they collected their EKG data:

> For all participants, the electrocardiograph (EKG) was recorded from solid-gelled Ag–AgCl disposable electrodes through an AC amp from Contact Precision Instruments. Low-pass and high-pass filters were set to 30 and 0.3 Hz, respectively. All data were digitized online at 100 Hz (128 Hz in the earlier study). All physiological data were acquired with software from Contact Precision Instruments running on an IBM-compatible computer. (Taylor & James, 2009, p. 493)

Each biometric marker will have a unique set of parameters that need to be reported. As with psychological measures, the JARS recommends that enough information be provided to allow others to judge the adequacy of the measures and to replicate results.

Research Design

The Method section must also contain information on your research design and the procedures you used to implement it. Elsewhere, I have discussed the basic issues involved in the choice of a research design (Cooper, 2006). Briefly, three principal questions need to be asked to determine the appropriateness of a design for answering a research question:

- Should the results of the research be expressed in numbers or narrative?
- Is the problem you are studying a description of an event, an association between events, or a causal explanation of an event?
- Does the problem or hypothesis address (a) how a process unfolds within an individual participant over time or (b) what is associated with or explains variation between participants or groups of participants?

Your description of the research design should include

- whether conditions were manipulated (Table A1.2) or naturally observed and
- the type of research design; provided in Table A1.3 are modules for randomized experiments (Module A1) and quasi-experiments (Module A2).

(Other designs would have different reporting needs associated with them.)

The JARS material on research designs currently covers only designs that seek quantitative causal explanations. It speaks to only two variations of a design in which conditions are experimentally or purposively manipulated to examine the effects of the manipulations on selected outcome or dependent variables. Within this type of design, participants can be assigned to conditions either randomly or nonrandomly—for example, through self- or administrative selection. Our hypothetical study involving the effects of labeling perfume (Roses vs. Manure) would be an experiment with random assignment.

That said, the variety of designs illustrated in the examples I have given demonstrate that the JARS items covering participants' characteristics, sampling procedures, power analysis, and measurement characteristics relate to all studies regardless of the researchers' answers to the three questions related to research design, as does the material in the previous chapter and the chapters that follow. As noted in Chapter 1, different research designs have different reporting needs, and one hopes that standards for them will emerge over time. Regardless, an extremely important JARS recommendation is that your report include a description of the research design, one that will allow readers to decide whether the design you have chosen and the way it was implemented allow you to draw the inferences you desire.

Reporting Standards for Studies With Experimental Manipulations or Interventions

If your study involved an experimental manipulation or intervention (Table A1.2), your report should describe details of the interventions or experimental manipulations intended for each study condition, including control groups, and how and when manipulations or interventions were actually administered, specifically including:

■ the content of the interventions or specific experimental manipulations (summary or paraphrasing of instructions, unless they are unusual or compose the experimental manipulation, in which case they may be presented verbatim), and
■ the method of manipulation or intervention delivery, including
   ■ a description of apparatus and materials used and their function in the experiment, such as specialized equipment by model and supplier.

The JARS recommends that research reports contain detailed descriptions of all of the different conditions that participants were exposed to in studies with experimental manipulations. To illustrate the different items on the JARS, I use two different examples.

The first example is from an article by Vinnars, Thormählen, Gallop, Norén, and Barber (2009) titled "Do Personality Problems Improve During Psychodynamic Supportive–Expressive Psychotherapy? Secondary Outcome Results From a Randomized Controlled Trial for Psychiatric Outpatients With Personality Disorders," published in *Psychotherapy: Theory, Research, Practice, Training.*[8] In this study, two treatments for personality disorder were compared. The experimental treatment was a manualized version of supportive–expressive psychotherapy (SEP), and the control condition was nonmanualized community-delivered psychodynamic treatment (CDPT). Thus, this was a simple one-factor between-subjects design with two experimental conditions.

The second example is from an article by Adank, Evans, Stuart-Smith, and Scott (2009) titled "Comprehension of Familiar and Unfamiliar Native Accents Under Adverse Listening Conditions," published in the *Journal of Experimental Psychology: Human Perception and Performance.* The researchers created two groups of listeners. One group of listeners was drawn from the residents of London, England. They heard taped sentences spoken in standard English (SE) or Glaswegian English (GE) and were assumed to be familiar with the former but unfamiliar with the latter. The second group of listeners was drawn from Glasgow, Scotland, and listened to the same tapes but was assumed to be familiar with both accents (because of media exposure). Also, noise at three volumes was added to the tapes to create four conditions of noise (one being a no-noise condition). Therefore, there were eight experimental conditions. In their overview of their design, Adank et al. also informed readers that

> 96 true/false sentences were presented to the participants, that is, 12 sentences per experimental condition. The sentences were counterbalanced across conditions, so that all 96 sentences were presented in all conditions across all

[8]Is this title too wordy according to JARS recommendations? Can you make it shorter? Does the descriptor *randomized controlled trial* need to be in the title, or could this be mentioned in the abstract?

subjects within a listener group. All listeners heard sentences in all four conditions. This was repeated for the SE and GE listener groups, thus ensuring that
all sentences were presented in all conditions for both groups. Furthermore, not
more than two sentences of one speaker were presented in succession, as
Clarke and Garrett (2004) found that familiarization occurs after as few as two
sentences from a speaker. (p. 521)

Thus, Adank et al. used a two-factor (2 × 4) within-subjects experimental design with
an additional individual difference, whether the participant spoke SE or GE, serving as
a between-subjects factor.

I chose these two studies because they are so different in both focus and setting.
The first study was an attempt to assess the effectiveness of a clinical treatment applied
in community mental health centers. The second focused on perceptual processes and
was conducted in a laboratory. Because of these differences, the two studies can be used
to highlight different aspects of the JARS recommendations.

Details of the treatment or experimental manipulation. Vinnars et al. (2009) used a manualized version of their psychotherapy manipulation, so we should not be surprised to
find that their description of it begins with reference to where the manuals can be found:

> The SEP in this study followed Luborsky's treatment manual (Barber & Crits-
> Christoph, 1995; Luborsky, 1984). The treatment consisted of 40 sessions
> delivered, on average, over the course of 1 calendar year. (p. 365)

Vinnars et al. (2009) sent us elsewhere to find the details of their experimental treatment. This is a perfectly appropriate reporting approach, as long as (a) the document
referred to is easily available (e.g., has been published, is available on the Internet), (b) the
conceptual underpinnings of the treatment were carefully detailed (as they were in
Vinnars et al.'s, 2009, introduction), and (c) any details are reported regarding how the
treatment was implemented that might be different from the manual description or not
be contained therein. This description also contains information on the exposure quantity (40 treatment sessions) and the time span of the treatment (about 1 calendar year).
Perhaps more interesting is the researchers' description of the comparison group:

> The comparison group was intended to be a naturalistic treatment as usual for
> PD [personality disorder] patients. The basic psychotherapeutic training of these
> clinicians was psychoanalytically oriented, and they received supervision from a
> psychoanalyst during the study period. They were not provided with any clinical
> guidelines on how to treat their patients. They chose their own preferred treat-
> ments and had the freedom to determine the focus of the treatment, its fre-
> quency, and when to terminate treatment. However, it was quite clear that
> the predominant orientation of all but one therapist was psychodynamic. This
> reinforced our conclusion that this trial involved the comparison of two psycho-
> dynamic treatments, one manualized and time limited and one nonmanualized.
> (Vinnars et al., 2009, p. 365)

In evaluation research conducted in naturalistic settings, the comparison group
often receives "treatment as usual." Many times, this creates a problem for readers and

potential replicators of the study findings because they have no way of knowing exactly what the comparison treatment was. The effect of a treatment is as much dependent on what it is being compared against as on what the treatment is. After all, even the effect of different perfume labels depends on both labels (Roses vs. Manure as opposed to Roses vs. Daisies). If your control group receives treatment as usual, consider in your research design how you will collect information on what usual treatment is. This may involve observing the control group and/or giving treatment deliverers and control group members additional questions about what they did or what happened to them. The important point is that just collecting the outcome variables from control group members typically will not be enough for you (and your readers) to interpret the meaning of any group differences you find. To address this problem, the JARS explicitly asks for descriptions of the control groups and how they were treated. Vinnars et al. (2009) described this; be sure to do the same.

Methods of manipulation or intervention delivery. The methods and materials used by Adank et al. (2009) to deliver the spoken sentences in their study involved, first, the creation of the spoken sentences stimulus materials. This is the material that Vinnars et al. (2009) told readers they could find in the SEP manuals associated with their study. Adank et al. had no manuals to refer to, so the amount of detail they gave is impressive. First, Adank et al. described how the tapes were made to ensure that only the speakers' accents varied across the spoken sentences:

> For every speaker, recordings were made of the 100 sentences of Version A of the SCOLP [Speed and Capacity of Language Processing] test (Baddeley et al., 1992). The sentence was presented on the screen of a notebook computer, and speakers were instructed to quietly read the sentence and subsequently to pronounce the sentence as a declarative statement. All sentences were recorded once. However, if the speaker made a mistake, the interviewer went back two sentences, and the speaker was instructed to repeat both. . . .
>
> The GE speakers were recorded in a sound-treated room, using an AKG SE300B microphone (AKG Acoustics, Vienna, Austria), which was attached to an AKG N6-6E preamplifier, on a Tascam DA-P1 DAT recorder (Tascam Div., TEAC Corp., Tokyo, Japan). Each stimulus was transferred directly to hard disk using a Kay Elemetrics DSP sonagraph (Kay Elemetrics, Lincoln Park, NJ). . . . The recordings of the SE speakers were made in an anechoic room, using a Brüel and Kjær 2231 sound level meter (Brüel and Kjær Sound & Vibration Measurement, Nærum, Denmark) as a microphone/amplifier. This microphone was fitted with a 4165 microphone cartridge and its A/C output was fed to the line input of a Sony 60ES DAT recorder (Sony Corp., Tokyo) and the digital output from the DAT recorder fed to the digital input of a Delta 66 sound card (M-Audio UK, Watford, UK) in the Dell Optiplex GX280 personal computer (Dell Corp., Fort Lauderdale, FL). . . . The difference in recording conditions between the two speaker groups was not noticeable in the recordings, and it is thus unlikely that intelligibility of the two accents was affected.
>
> Next, all sentences were saved into their own file with beginning and end trimmed at zero crossings (trimming on or as closely as possible to the onset and offset of initial and final speech sounds) and resampled at 22,050 Hz.

Subsequently, the speech rate differences across all eight speakers were equalized, so that every sentence had the same length across all eight speakers. This was necessary to ensure straightforward interpretation of the dependent variable (i.e., to be able to express the results in milliseconds). First, for each of the 96 sentences, the average duration across all speakers was calculated. Second, we used the Pitch Synchronous Overlap Add Method, or PSOLA (Moulines & Charpentier, 1990), as implemented in the Praat software package (Boersma & Weenink, 2003), to digitally shorten or lengthen the sentence for each speaker separately. The effect of the shortening or lengthening was in some cases just audible, but it was expected that any effects due to this manipulation were small to negligible, as the manipulations were relatively small and were carried out across all sentences for all speakers in the experiment. (p. 522)

This level of detail is called for in the *Publication Manual*:

> If a mechanical apparatus was used to present stimulus materials or collect data, include in the description of procedures the apparatus model number and manufacturer (when important, as in neuroimaging studies), its key settings or parameters (e.g., pulse settings), and its resolution (e.g., regarding stimulus delivery, recording precision). (APA, 2010b, p. 31)

The level of detail also suggests that this area of research is probably working with very subtle and sensitive effects (note the attention to the speed of speech). This requires of the experimenters a great deal of control of what and how stimulus materials are presented to produce it. Note that Adank et al. also mentioned the locations (London and Glasgow) at which the recordings for the experiment took place.

Adank et al. (2009) then went on to describe how they accomplished the noise manipulation:

> Finally, speech-shaped noise was added. . . . This speech-shaped noise was based on an approximation to the long-term average speech spectrum for combined male and female voices. . . . The root-mean-square levels per one third of the octave band were converted into spectrum level and plotted on an octave scale. A three-line approximation was used to capture the major part of the shape from 60 Hz to 9 kHz. This consisted of a low-frequency portion rolling off below 120 Hz at 17.5 dB/octave and a high-frequency portion rolling off at 7.2 dB/octave above 420 Hz, with a constant spectrum portion in between. Per sentence, the noise sound file was cut at a random position from a longer (6-s) segment of speech-shaped noise, so that the noise varied randomly across sentences. The speech-shaped noise had the same duration as the sentence and started and ended with the onset and offset of the sentence. The root mean squares of the sentence and the noise were determined and scaled as to fit the SNR [signal-to-noise ratio] level and finally were combined through addition. Finally, using Praat, we peak-normalized and scaled the intensity of the sound file to 70 dB sound pressure level (SPL). (p. 522)

If your study involved an experimental manipulation or intervention, your report should describe

- deliverers: who delivered the manipulations or interventions (level of professional training, level of training in the specific manipulations or interventions, number of deliverers and, in the case of interventions, the mean, standard deviation, and range of number of individuals/units treated by each);
- setting: where the manipulations or interventions occurred;
- exposure quantity and duration: how many sessions, episodes, or events were intended to be delivered, how long they were intended to last;
- time span: how long it took to deliver the manipulation or intervention to each unit;
- activities to increase compliance or adherence (e.g., incentives); and
- use of language other than English and the translation method.

Deliverers. In Vinnars et al.'s (2009) study, the experimental and comparison interventions were delivered by psychotherapists. So, as the JARS recommends, the researchers paid careful attention in their Method section to the professional training of these treatment deliverers:

> Six psychologists conducted the SEP, and 21 clinicians performed the CDPT treatment. Three senior SEP therapists, with more than 20 years of experience in psychiatry and dynamic psychotherapy, had trained the remaining SEP therapists, whose experience varied from 1 to 10 years. The three senior SEP therapists had received their training in both SEP and the use of the adherence/competence rating scale . . . by the developers of the treatment. The training cases of these three therapists were translated into English and rated by adherence raters at the University of Pennsylvania Center for Psychotherapy Research until they reached acceptable adherence levels to start training the other SEP therapists and adherence raters in Sweden.
>
> The CDPT clinicians had a mean experience of 12.5 years in psychiatry and dynamic psychotherapy. All therapists except one had at least 1 year of full-time formal postgraduate training in dynamic psychotherapy consistent with a psychotherapist certification. They all received weekly psychodynamic psychotherapy supervision prior to and during the study. Within the public health care system, dynamic therapists tend to emphasize supportive techniques when dealing with patients with severe pathology. The CDPT group included two psychiatrists who had three patients in treatment, six psychologists who had 13 patients in treatment, five psychiatric nurses who had 42 patients in treatment, six psychiatric social workers who had 16 patients in treatment, and two psychiatric nurses' assistants who had two patients in treatment. All therapists were unaware of the specific hypotheses. (Vinnars et al., 2009, p. 365)

Vinnars et al. (2009) discussed the therapists' training in the specific SEP therapy when they described the treatment itself:

> All therapy sessions were videotaped, and two trained raters evaluated adherence to the SEP method using an adherence/competence scale. . . .
>
> Although the manualized SEP was time limited, CDPT was open ended. That is, the research team did not determine the length of treatment in the CDPT group. However, this did not mean that all CDPT patients received long-term therapy. In fact, the mean number of total treatment sessions attended between pretreatment and the 1-year follow-up assessment did not differ between the two groups (Mann–Whitney $U = 2{,}994.00$, $p < .87$). On average, SEP patients received 26 sessions ($SD = 15.2$, $Mdn = 30$, range = 0–78) and CDPT patients received 28 sessions ($SD = 23.7$, $Mdn = 22$, range = 0–101). Even when one focuses only on the time between the pretreatment and posttreatment assessments, the SEP patients had a mean of 25 ($SD = 13.0$, $Mdn = 30$, range = 0–40) sessions in contrast to 22 sessions for the CDPT patients ($SD = 15.5$, $Mdn = 21$, range = 0–61), respectively (Mann–Whitney $U = 2{,}638.00$, $p < .19$). (pp. 365–366)

For Adank et al. (2009), the equivalent deliverers of the treatment might be considered the people whose voices were recorded:

> Recordings were made of four SE speakers and four GE speakers. All speakers were male, middle class, and between 20 and 46 years old. Only male speakers were selected because including both genders would have introduced unwanted variation related to the gender differences in larynx size and vocal tract length. . . . The GE speakers were recorded in Glasgow, and the SE speakers were recorded in London. (p. 522)

Taking extra precaution, these researchers also described the persons helping the speakers create the tapes:

> Because our investigative team speaks in Southern English accents, we arranged for the GE recordings to be conducted by a native GE interviewer to avoid the possibility of speech accommodation toward Southern English (Trudgill, 1986). . . . The SE recordings were conducted by a native SE interviewer. (Adank et al., 2009, p. 522)

The level of detail these authors provide for how their experimental conditions were delivered is impressive. What might seem like trivial detail to an outsider can be critical to enabling someone immersed in this field to draw strong causal inferences from a study. How will you know what these details are? By reading the detailed reports of those who have done work in your area before you.

Setting. Adank et al.'s (2009) description of the experimental procedures focused on the physical characteristics of the experimental room, the mode of the manipulation delivery, and what participants had to do to respond:

> *Procedure.* The SE listeners were tested in London, and the GE listeners were tested in Glasgow. All listeners were tested individually in a quiet room while

facing the screen of a notebook computer. They received written instructions. The listeners responded using the notebook's keyboard. Half of the participants were instructed to press the *q* key with their left index finger for true responses and to press the *p* key with their right index finger for false responses. The response keys were reversed (i.e., *p* for true and *q* for false) for the other half of the participants. Listeners were not screened for handedness. The stimuli were presented over headphones (Philips SBC HN110; Philips Electronics, Eindhoven, the Netherlands) at a sound level that was kept constant for all participants. Stimulus presentation and the collection of the responses were performed with Cogent 2000 software (Cogent 2000 team, Wellcome Trust, London, UK), running under Matlab (Mathworks, Cambridge, UK). The response times were measured relative to the end of the audio file, following the computerized SCOLP task in May et al. (2001).

Each trial proceeded as follows. First, the stimulus sentence was presented. Second, the program waited for 3.5 s before playing the next stimulus, allowing the participant to make a response. If the participant did not respond within 3.5 s, the trial was recorded as *no response.* The participants were asked to respond as quickly as they could and told that they did not have to wait until the sentence had finished (allowing for negative response times, as response time was calculated from the offset of the sound file).

Ten familiarization trials were presented prior to the start of the experiment. The familiarization sentences had been produced by a male SE speaker. This speaker was not included in the actual experiment, and neither were the 10 familiarization sentences. The experiment's duration was 15 min, without breaks. (pp. 522–523)

In contrast, Vinnars et al. (2009) spent little space on the setting. We know the therapies were administered in community-based mental health facilities, and as such they varied in naturalistic ways. For these researchers, the characteristics of the therapists (included in the earlier excerpt) were important and would be most critical to interpreting and replicating their results.

Activities to increase compliance or adherence. Adank et al. (2009) told readers that the participants in their study were recruited from London and Glasgow and that "all were paid for their participation" (p. 522). Vinnars et al. (2009) said that participants were recruited from two community mental health centers and had either self-applied or been referred for treatment. They had a compliance problem in that participants in the SEP condition entered into contracts before the treatment began, but CDPT participants did not. Here is how they reported on the problem:

Treatment Attendance

As the nonmanualized treatment, by its nature, did not have a protocol on which treatment contracts were agreed, the definition of dropouts for this condition was complicated. To solve the attendance issue, we collected session data from patients' medical records. Treatment attendance was classified into (a) regular once a week (SEP = 52, 65.0%; CDPT = 43, 56.6%); (b) irregular, that is, less frequent than once a week, including an inability to keep regular appointments scheduled once a week (SEP = 16, 20.0%; CDPT = 17, 22.4%); or (c) no treatment, that is, not attending more than two sessions after randomization (SEP = 12, 15.0%; CDPT = 16, 21.1%). No significant difference was found between the two treatments in terms of attendance, $\chi^2(2) = 1.35$, $p = .51$ (Vinnars et al., 2005). (Vinnars et al., 2009, p. 366)

Language. In Adank et al.'s (2009) study, the use of language other than SE was one of the experimental manipulations. The JARS recommends (see Table A1.2) that the research report indicate whether the language used to conduct the study was other than English. According to the *Publication Manual*,

When an instrument is translated into a language other than the language in which it was developed, describe the specific method of translation (e.g., back-translation, in which a text is translated into another language and then back into the first to ensure that it is equivalent enough that results can be compared). (APA, 2010b, p. 32)

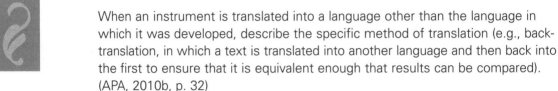

With regard to your units of delivery and analysis, your report should describe the unit of delivery or how participants were grouped during delivery, including

- description of the smallest unit that was analyzed (and, in the case of experiments, that was randomly assigned to conditions) to assess manipulation or intervention effects (e.g., individuals, work groups, classes) and
- if the unit of analysis differed from the unit of delivery, description of the analytical method used to account for this (e.g., adjusting the standard error estimates by the design effect or using multilevel analysis).

Unit of delivery and analysis. The JARS calls for a description of how participants were grouped during delivery. Was the manipulation administered individual by individual; to small or large groups; or to intact, naturally occurring groups? It also recommends that you describe the smallest unit you used in your data analysis.

The reason for recommending that this information be reported goes beyond the reader's need to know the method of manipulation delivery and analysis. In most instances, the unit of delivery and the unit of analysis need to be the same for the assumptions of statistical tests to be met. Specifically at issue is the assumption that each data point in the analysis is independent of the other data points. When participants are tested in groups, it is possible that the individuals in each group affect one another in ways that would influence their scores on the dependent variable.

Suppose you conducted your labeling study by having 10 groups of five participants each smell the fragrance when it was labeled Roses and another 10 groups of five participants each smell it when it was labeled Manure. Before you had participants rate the fragrances, you allowed them to engage in a group discussion. The discussions might have gone very differently in different groups. The first person to speak up in one of the manure groups might have framed the discussion for the entire group by stating, "I would never buy a fragrance called Manure!" whereas in another group, the first speaker might have said, "Manure! What a bold marketing strategy!" Such comments could lower and raise, respectively, all group members' ratings. Therefore, the ratings within groups are no longer independent. By knowing the participants' groups, you know something about whether their ratings will be lower or higher than those of other participants not in their group, even within the manure and roses conditions.

This example, of course, is unlikely to happen (I hope); clearly, participants should complete this type of labeling study individually, unless the research question deals with the influence of groups on labeling (in which case the framing comments likely would also be experimentally manipulated). However, there are many instances in which treatments are applied to groups formed purposively (e.g., group therapy) or naturalistically (e.g., classrooms). Still, in many of these instances, there will be a temptation to conduct the data analysis with the individual participant as the unit of analysis, either because (a) the analysis is simpler or (b) using the participant as the unit of analysis increases the power of the test by increasing the available degrees of freedom. In your labeling experiment run in groups, there are 100 participants but only 20 groups.

Some data analysis techniques take into account the potential dependence of scores within groups (Luke, 2004). If you used such an analytic method, describe it. Describing these techniques here goes beyond the scope of this discussion; for now, it is only important that you understand the rationale behind why the JARS asks for this information.

A study that addressed the issue of units of delivery and analysis, "Repeated Reading Intervention: Outcomes and Interactions With Readers' Skills and Classroom Instruction," was conducted by Vadasy and Sanders (2008) and appeared in the *Journal of Educational Psychology*. This study examined the effects of a reading intervention on second and third graders' reading fluency. The intervention was delivered in groups of two students. Here is how the researchers described their method of composing the units of delivery:

> Group assignment was a two-stage process. First, eligible students were randomly assigned to dyads (pairs of students) within grade and school using a random number generator. Although it would have been preferable to randomly assign students to dyads within classrooms in order to minimize extreme mismatches between students within a dyad, there were too few eligible students within classrooms to make this practical. Nevertheless, there were sufficient numbers of eligible students for random assignment of dyads within grades (within schools). For schools with uneven numbers of students within grades, we used random selection to identify singletons that were subsequently excluded from participation. Dyads were then randomly assigned to one of two conditions: treatment (supplemental fluency tutoring instruction) or control (no tutoring; classroom instruction only). (Vadasy & Sanders, 2008, p. 274)

They went on to describe their unit of analysis and the rationale for their choice of data analysis strategy by simply stating,

> Due to nesting structures present in our research design, a multilevel (hierarchical) modeling approach was adopted for analyzing group differences on pretests and gains. (Vadasy & Sanders, 2008, p. 280)

Reporting Randomized Field or Clinical Trials

If you used random assignment (Table A1.3, Module A1) to place participants into experimental conditions, your description should include

- procedures used to generate the random assignment sequence, including details of any restrictions (e.g., blocking, stratification),
- concealment (whether sequence was concealed until the interventions were assigned), and
- implementation (who generated the assignment sequence, who enrolled participants, and who assigned participants to groups).

If you used an assignment method other than random assignment (Table A1.3, Module A2) to place participants into experimental conditions, you should describe

- the unit of assignment (the unit being assigned to study conditions, e.g., individual, group, community) and
- the method used to assign units to study conditions, including details of any restriction (e.g., blocking, stratification, minimization) procedures used to help minimize potential bias due to nonrandomization (e.g., matching, propensity score matching).

Knowing whether participants have been assigned to conditions in a study at random or through some self-choice or administrative procedure is critical to readers' ability to understand the study's potential for revealing causal relationships. Random assignment makes it unlikely that there will be any differences between the experimental groups, on average, before the manipulation occurs (Boruch, 1997). If participants are placed into experimental groups using random assignment, then, when group averages are compared prior to manipulation, we can assume that they do not differ on characteristics that might be related to the dependent variable.[9] In the case of self- or administrative selection into groups, it is quite plausible that the groups will differ on many dimensions before the manipulation is introduced, and some of these dimensions are likely related to the dependent variable. This compromises the ability of studies using self- or administrative assignment techniques to lead to strong causal inferences about the manipulation. For example, if participants in the labeling study were first asked whether they would like to smell a fragrance called Roses or one called Manure and then they were assigned to their preference, there would be no way to determine whether their subsequent ratings of the fragrances were caused by a labeling effect or by individual differences participants brought with them to the study (perhaps more

---

[9]Of course, this does not rule out differences between groups arising after random assignment has occurred. For example, more participants assigned to smell a fragrance called Manure may choose not to complete the study than would those assigned to smell a fragrance called Roses. The decision to quit the study could be related to their predisposition to like the things they smell. This is called *differential attrition* and is discussed more fully in Chapter 4. Also, sometimes random assignment fails simply because it is a chance process; by bad luck alone groups will be created that differ on the dependent variable.

participants in the manure condition grew up on a farm?). For this reason, studies using random assignment are called *experiments, randomized field trials,* or *randomized clinical trials,* whereas those using nonrandom assignment are called *quasi-experiments.*

Experiments. It is essential that your report tell readers what procedure you used to assign participants to conditions. When random assignment is used in a laboratory context, it is often okay to say only that random assignment happened. However, you can add how the random assignment sequence was generated, for example, by using a random numbers table, an urn randomization method, or a statistical package.

Your study may also have involved a more sophisticated random assignment technique. For example, when the number of participants in an experiment is small, it is often good practice to first create groups that include a number of participants equal to the number of conditions in the study and then to randomly assign one member of the group to each condition. This technique, called *blocking,* ensures that you end up with equal numbers of participants in each condition.

Sometimes *stratified random assignment* is used to ensure that groups are equal across important strata of participants, for example, using the blocking strategy to assign each pair of women and each pair of men to the two labeling conditions. In this way, you can ensure that the roses and manure conditions have equal numbers of participants of each sex. This is important if you think fragrance ratings will differ between sexes. If your study uses such a technique, say so in your report.

Method of concealment. The next JARS recommendation concerns the issue of concealment of the allocation process. It raises the issue of whether the person enrolling people in a study knows which condition is coming up next. In most psychology laboratory experiments, this is of little importance; the enrollment is done by computer. In field settings, this might not be the case, however. For example, if we were enrolling participants in Vinnars et al.'s (2009) study of SEP therapy versus treatment as usual, we would not want to steer people into or out of the study on the basis of whether we felt the participant would benefit from the treatment that was next to be assigned. This is why Vinnars et al. reported both that "patients were randomized using a computerized stratification randomization procedure" (p. 368) and that "participants were consecutively recruited from two community mental health centers" (p. 364). The word *consecutively* indicates that participants were screened only on whether they had a personality disorder; the enroller had no personal leeway in deciding whom to invite into the study. Similarly, who generates the assignment sequence, who enrolls participants, and who assigns participants to groups need to be reported in experiments in which some form of bias in recruiting and assignment might creep into the process at each of these time points.

Quasi-experiments. When a nonrandom process is used to assign participants to conditions, some other technique typically will be used to make the groups as equivalent as possible (see Shadish, Cook, & Campbell, 2002, for how this is done). Frequently used techniques include (a) matching people across the groups on important dimensions and removing the data of participants who do not have a good match and (b) post hoc statistical control of variables believed related to the outcome measure, using an analysis of covariance or multiple regression.

Evers, Brouwers, and Tomic (2006) provided an example of reporting a quasi-experiment in their article "A Quasi-Experimental Study on Management Coaching Effectiveness," published in *Consulting Psychology Journal: Practice and Research.* In this study, the experimental group was composed of managers who had signed up (self-selected) to be coached. Evers et al. were then faced with constructing a no-coaching comparison group. Here is how they described the process:

The Experimental Group

We asked staff managers of various departments which managers were about to be coached. . . . We got the names of 41 managers who were about to register for coaching; 30 managers agreed to participate in our quasi-experiment, 19 men (63.3%) and 11 women (36.7%). Their ages ranged between 27 and 53 years ($M = 38.8$; $SD = 8.20$). The mean number of years as a manager was 5.34 years ($SD = 5.66$), and the mean number of years in the present position was 1.76 years ($SD = 2.52$).

The Control Group

We asked 77 managers of the Department of Housing and Urban Development to fill up our questionnaires: Of this group, 22 did not respond, whereas 48 of them answered the questionnaires both at the beginning and at the end of our quasi-experiment. We matched the groups with the help of salary scales, for these scales of the federal government are indicative of the weight of a position. We also matched the groups as much as possible according to sex and age, which ultimately resulted in a control group of 30 managers, of which 20 (66.7%) were men and 10 (33.3%) were women. Their ages ranged from 26 to 56 years, with a mean of 43.6 years ($SD = 8.31$), which means that the mean age of the control group is 4.8 years older. The mean number of years as a manager was 8.64 years ($SD = 7.55$), which means that they worked 3.3 years longer in this position than members of the experimental group did. The members of the control group had been working in the present position for a mean of 2.76 years ($SD = 2.39$), which is 1 year more than the members of the experimental group.

The experimental and the control groups . . . were equal on sex, $\chi^2(1) = 0.14$, $p = .71$; the number of years as a manager, $t(58) = 1.91$, $p = .06$; and the total number of years in the present position, $t(58) = 1.58$, $p = .12$; but not on age, $t(58) = 2.25$, $p = .03$. (Evers et al., 2006, pp. 176–177)

First, as recommended in the JARS, it is clear from Evers et al.'s (2006) description that the individual manager was the unit of assignment. The first sentence tells readers that participants had not been randomly assigned to the coaching condition; the method of assignment was self-choice or administrative selection. We do not know (and I suspect the researchers did not either) whether participants requested coaching or were nominated for it (or both), but the managers in the coaching group are clearly people who could be different from all managers in numerous ways: They might have needed coaching because of poor job performance, or they might have been good managers who were highly motivated to become even better. The group of not-coached managers who were invited to take part was chosen because they had similar salaries. The researchers told readers that 77 other managers were asked to be in the control group, of whom 48 provided the necessary data (these numbers relate more to our assessment of the representativeness of control group managers than to issues related to condition assignment). Then, within the responding invitees, further matching was done on the basis of the manager's sex and age. This resulted in a control group of 30, comprising the best matches for the managers in the coached group. Finally, Evers et al. informed readers that their matching procedure produced groups that were equivalent in sex and experience but not in age. The researchers found that coached managers had some higher outcome expectancies and self-efficacy beliefs. Because the coached and not-coached groups also differed in age, is it possible that managers score higher on these two variables simply because these two self-beliefs grow more positive as a function of growing older?

If you used masking, you should

- report whether participants, those administering the interventions, and those assessing the outcomes were unaware of condition assignments; and
- include a statement regarding how masking was accomplished and how the success of masking was evaluated.

Masking. As the JARS states, *masking* refers to whether participants, those administering the interventions or experimental manipulations, and those assessing the outcomes were unaware of which condition each participant was in. Masking is most likely to take place in circumstances in which knowledge of the condition could itself influence the behavior of the participant or the person interacting with him or her. In the perfume labeling experiment, for example, participants should not know that there is also another condition in which people are reacting to a fragrance called something else. Otherwise they might react to their assignment ("Why did I have to smell Manure?") rather than the fragrance itself. The person interacting with the participant should not know what the label is for this participant; this knowledge might influence how the person behaves, either wittingly or unwittingly (e.g., smiling more at participants in the roses condition). Also, if you had someone rate, say, the facial expression of participants after sniffing the fragrance, you would want the rater to be unaware of the participants' condition to guard against a possible bias in his or her rating.

Masking used to be referred to as *blinding,* and it is still not unusual to see reference to *single-blind* and *double-blind* experiments. The first refers to a study in which participants do not know which condition they are in, and the second refers to a study in which neither the participant nor the experimenter knows the condition.[10] For example, Amir et al.'s (2009) article "Attention Training in Individuals With Generalized Social Phobia: A Randomized Controlled Trial" was discussed earlier for its power analysis. This was a study in which all parties who could introduce bias

---

[10]The term *blinding* was abandoned by APA in the mid-1980s because it used a description of a disability in a metaphoric sense. Even though the term has not been used in APA guidelines for more than 2 decades, it still appears in some APA journals. Personally, I don't like *masking* either and use *were kept unaware* as an alternative.

were kept unaware of condition assignment. Clinicians rated some outcome measures and did not know whether the participants received the experimental treatment or placebo:

Measures

We used a battery of clinician- and self-rated measures at pre- and postassessment. Clinician ratings were made by raters blind to treatment condition. (Amir et al., 2009, p. 964)

Also, participants and experimenters were kept unaware of the participants' condition:

Procedure

Prior to each experimental session, participants entered the number in their file into the computer. . . . Participants did not know which condition the numbers represented, and the research assistants working with the participants could not see the number in the envelope. Thus, participants, experimenters, and interviewers remained blind to a participant's condition until all posttreatment assessments had been conducted. (Amir et al., 2009, p. 965)

Further, the researchers assessed whether their procedure to keep participants unaware of their condition was successful:

To assess whether participants remained blind to their respective experimental condition, we asked participants at postassessment whether they thought they had received the active versus placebo intervention. Of the participants who provided responses, 21% (4/19) of participants in the AMP and 28% (5/18) of ACC participants thought they had received the active treatment, $\chi^2(1, N = 37) = 0.23$, $p = .63$. These findings bolster confidence that participants did not systematically predict their respective experimental condition. (Amir et al., 2009, p. 965)

Amir et al. (2009) also pointed out in their discussion two limitations of the masking procedures they used:

Follow-up data should be interpreted with caution because assessors and participants were no longer blind to participant condition. . . .
   We did not collect data regarding interviewers' or experimental assistants' guesses regarding participants' group assignment and therefore cannot definitively establish that interviewers and assistants remained blind to participant condition in all cases. (pp. 969–971)

From these descriptions, it is easy for the reader to assess whether knowledge of the treatment condition might have affected the study's outcomes (unlikely, I suspect) and for replicators to know what they need to do to reproduce or improve on what Amir et al. did.

If you used random assignment, with regard to statistical methods, your report should describe

- statistical methods used to compare groups on primary outcome(s);
- statistical methods used for additional analyses, such as subgroup analyses and adjusted analyses; and
- statistical methods used for mediation analyses.

If nonrandom assignment placed participants in groups, with regard to statistical methods, your report should describe

- statistical methods used to compare study groups on primary outcome(s), including complex methods for correlated data;
- statistical methods used for additional analyses, such as subgroup analyses and adjusted analyses (e.g., methods for modeling pretest differences and adjusting for them); and
- statistical methods used for mediation analyses.

Statistical analyses. Many research reports conclude the Method section with a subsection titled "Statistical Analysis" or "Analysis Strategy," or some variation thereof. Sometimes this is presented as a subsection of the Results section. Other times, the description of each analysis strategy appears in the Results section just before the results of that analysis are described. Regardless of where it appears, you should lay out the broad strategy you used to analyze your data and give the rationale for your choices.

As an example of how the analysis strategy might be described in a study using nonexperimental data, here is how Tsaousides et al. (2009) described their two-step analytic approach in their study of employment belief and brain injury:

Data Analysis

First, correlations were conducted to explore the relationship among demographic, injury related, employment, predictor (PEM and IND [Independence subscale of the Bigelow Quality of Life Questionnaire]), and outcome variables (PQoL [perceived quality of life] and UIN [unmet important needs]). Subsequently, two hierarchical regression analyses were conducted, to determine the relevant contribution of each predictor to each outcome variable. In addition to the predictor variables, all demographic variables that correlated moderately ($r \geq .20$) with either outcome variable and all injury-related variables were included in the regression analysis. . . . Employment status was included in both regression analyses as well, to compare the predictive value of employment to the self-efficacy variables. (p. 302)

Amir et al. (2009) provided an example of how to report the analytic strategy for an experiment using analysis of variance. The subsection on their statistical analysis of the study on attention training covered about a column of text. Here is a portion of what they wrote about their primary measures:

To examine the effect of the attention training procedure on the dependent variables, we submitted participants' scores on self-report and interviewer measures to a series of 2 (group: AMP [attention modification program], ACC [attention control condition]) × 2 (time: preassessment, postassessment) ANOVAs [analyses of variance] with repeated measurement on the second factor. Multivariate ANOVAs were used for conceptually related measures . . . and a univariate ANOVA was used for disability ratings. . . . Significant multivariate effects were followed up with corresponding univariate tests. We followed up significant interactions with within-group simple effects analyses (*t* tests) as well as analyses of covariance on posttreatment scores covarying pretreatment scores to determine whether the AMP resulted in a significant change on the relevant dependent measures from pre- to postassessment. . . . A series of 2 (group) × 2 (time) × 2 (site: UGA [University of Georgia], SDSU [San Diego State University]) analyses established that there was no significant effect of site on the primary dependent measures (all *p*s > .20). The magnitude of symptom change was established by calculating (a) within-group effect sizes = (preassessment mean minus postassessment mean)/preassessment standard deviation, and (b) between-group controlled effect sizes = (postassessment ACC covariance adjusted mean minus postassessment AMP covariance adjusted mean)/pooled standard deviation. (Amir et al., 2009, pp. 966–967)

The researchers began by telling readers the variables of primary interest. Then they described how the initial data analysis mirrored the research design; there were two experimental groups with each participant measured at two times, so they had a 2 × 2 design with the time of measurement as a repeated-measures factor. They protected against an inflated experiment-wise error by grouping conceptually related variables and only followed up significant multivariate effects with univariate tests. Significant interactions (tests of potential mediators that might influence the strength of the effect of the treatment) were followed by simple tests of subgroups. They finished by telling readers how they calculated their effect sizes, in this case, standardized mean differences, or *d* indexes. This description perfectly matches the recommendations of the JARS.

Your Method section is now complete. In Chapter 4, I delve more deeply into what and how statistics are reported in the Results section of your research report.

4

Summarizing Your Data and Statistical Analyses: The Results Section

The Results section of your manuscript summarizes your data and the statistical analyses you applied to them. The rules here regarding completeness and transparency are the same as those you applied when reporting your method. According to the *Publication Manual* (APA, 2010b), you are obligated to report the data "in sufficient detail to justify your conclusions" (p. 32). The *Publication Manual* goes on to say, "Mention all relevant results, including those that run counter to expectation; be sure to include small effect sizes (or statistically nonsignificant findings) when theory predicts large (or statistically significant) ones. Do not hide uncomfortable results by omission" (p. 32).

The *Publication Manual* indicates that you do not need to include the individual scores or raw data in the report except when the study involved a single-case design or for purposes of illustration (and here only with proper protection against identifying the individual who provided the data, of course). However, the APA Ethics Code (APA, 2010a) encourages data sharing. Therefore, it is important for you to keep your data in interpretable fashion for at least 5 years after any report has been published. I have reproduced in Exhibit 4.1 the relevant section of the APA Ethics Code.

Also, if your research received support from a funding agency, governmental or otherwise, you may find that the funder obligates you to share your data with others if they ask or to make it publicly available on a certain date. Further, it is becoming more common for researchers to make their raw data available in online supplemental archives that are posted on the Internet, with a link provided in the published report.

> **■ Exhibit 4.1.**
>
> ## Entry in the *Ethical Principles of Psychologists and Code of Conduct* Relating to Data Sharing
>
> ### 8.14 Sharing Research Data for Verification
>
> (a) After research results are published, psychologists do not withhold the data on which their conclusions are based from other competent professionals who seek to verify the substantive claims through reanalysis and who intend to use such data only for that purpose, provided that the confidentiality of the participants can be protected and unless legal rights concerning proprietary data preclude their release. This does not preclude psychologists from requiring that such individuals or groups be responsible for costs associated with the provision of such information.
>
> (b) Psychologists who request data from other psychologists to verify the substantive claims through reanalysis may use shared data only for the declared purpose. Requesting psychologists obtain prior written agreement for all other uses of the data.
>
> *Note.* From *Ethical Principles of Psychologists and Code of Conduct* (2002, Amended June 1, 2010), p. 11, by the American Psychological Association, 2010, Washington, DC: Author. Copyright 2010 by the American Psychological Association.

Participants

> Your description of the flow of participants through your study should include
>
> ■ total number of participants and
> ■ the flow of participants through each stage of the study.

The first subsection of your results may be where you decide to report the changes in the number of participants at each stage of your study. I address issues related to participant flow in Chapter 3 of this volume, where I discuss the description of participant characteristics, because many researchers describe participant flow in the Method section. These researchers feel that describing the results of the sampling process along with the description of the intended population for the study and how this population was sampled presents a more coherent picture. Therefore, I do not present that material again. Instead, I review an example of the use of Figure A1.1, the Journal Article Reporting Standards (JARS) flowchart (APA Publications and Communications Board Working Group on Journal Article Reporting Standards, 2008), which is an adaptation of a flowchart in the CONSORT reporting guidelines (Altman et al., 2001; Moher, Schulz, & Altman, 2001) and is used by many journals in the medical field.

Figure 4.1 reproduces a participant flow diagram presented in Norman, Maley, Li, and Skinner's (2008) article "Using the Internet to Assist Smoking Prevention and

Figure 4.1. Diagram of Participants' Progress Through Phases of the Study

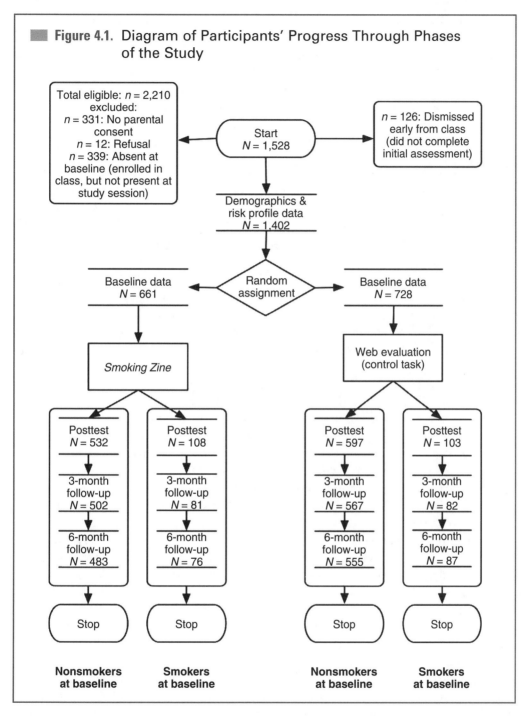

Adapted from "Using the Internet to Assist Smoking Prevention and Cessation in Schools: A Randomized, Controlled Trial," by C. D. Norman, O. Maley, X. Li, and H. A. Skinner, 2008, *Health Psychology, 27*, p. 802. Copyright 2008 by the American Psychological Association.

Cessation in Schools: A Randomized, Controlled Trial," published in *Health Psychology*. In the study, participants were randomly assigned to either a web-based tobacco intervention that involved a website called the *Smoking Zine* or a control task. Interventions occurred during a single classroom session with a follow-up by e-mail. The intervention website included interactive quizzes and self-assessments with feedback aimed at improving adolescents' resistance to pressure to smoke. In the control group, students did similar web-based activities unrelated to smoking cessation.

Attrition

The reason the JARS calls for a detailed description of participant progress through a study relates to the potential impact of attrition on the internal validity of a study, the external validity of a study, or both. *Attrition* is the loss of participants while a study is in progress (this is also sometimes referred to as *subject mortality*, but that term has fallen out of use, for obvious reasons).

Attrition from a study comes in two forms, *overall attrition* and *differential attrition* across conditions. A large amount of overall attrition often suggests that the study may lack external validity, that is, it does not produce results that generalize to certain subpopulations within the target population. For example, Figure 4.1, from Norman et al.'s (2008) study, shows that out of 2,210 eligible students, 331 did not obtain parental consent, and 339 were absent on the day of the experiment. Could these exclusions be related to student characteristics that distinguish them from participating students in important ways that relate to the effectiveness of the intervention? Here are some suggestions that are far-fetched but illustrate the thinking involved in assessing the effect of attrition on the generalizability of findings. Perhaps a lack of parental consent is related to whether the parent is a smoker. If so, the nonparticipating group might have been more likely to contain smokers who were most resistant to intervention, thus restricting the generality of findings to the least resistant students. What about the 126 students dismissed early from class? Could they share a characteristic (e.g., are they athletes?) that might relate to the generalizability of findings?

Differential attrition occurs when more people choose to leave a study from one condition than another. When this happens, even if random assignment was used, you have to wonder whether the groups would still be comparable on all variables other than the experimental manipulation. This is much like the self-selection into conditions that I have discussed in Chapter 3. Differential attrition, then, poses a threat to internal validity, or the experimenter's ability to draw strong causal inferences about the intervention. In Figure 4.1, one would examine the flow of smokers and nonsmokers through the two conditions from posttest to 6-month follow-up to decide whether differential attrition occurred. The attrition from conditions in Norman et al.'s (2008) study seems nonproblematic, but, again for illustrative purposes, note that 32 smokers were lost in the *Smoking Zine* condition, but only 16 were lost in the control condition. Is it possible that smokers for whom the intervention was less effective were unavailable at the 6-month follow-up? Could this have made the intervention look more effective than it might have had all of the smokers been available?

Here is how Vadasy and Sanders (2008) described the attrition problem in their repeated reading intervention evaluation in their article "Repeated Reading Intervention: Outcomes and Interactions With Readers' Skills and Classroom Instruction," published in the *Journal of Educational Psychology*:

Attrition. After group assignment, the sample comprised 96 students (48 dyads) in the treatment condition and 92 students (46 dyads) in the control condition. By the end of the study, 14 treatment and 12 control students were lost to attrition (14%). To ensure an operational definition of treatment as well as an unbiased attrition pattern across treatment and control groups, we removed any dyad member from study participation if the corresponding member moved from the school. (Although control pairs did not necessarily receive reading instruction together, we assumed that control pairs shared common reading curricula due to the within-grade, within-school pairings.) The sample used for analyses thus comprised 82 treatment students (41 dyads) and 80 control students (40 dyads). As reported in Table 1, there were no significant differences between groups on grade or status variable frequencies (all $ps > .05$). (pp. 274–275)

Note that the researchers made the case that differential attrition is not a problem by testing for differences among their experimental groups on some key variables.

Recruitment

> Your description of how you recruited participants should include dates defining the periods of recruitment and repeated measures or follow-up.

The dates of participant recruitment are also a detail that researchers often will include in the Method section rather than the Results section, sometimes along with the sampling procedures. Again, even though the dates are technically a description of the results of the study, presenting all of this information together may make it easier for readers to get the complete picture of the recruiting process (and, frankly, it is more important that the information be in your report somewhere than it be exactly where it is mentioned in the JARS). For example, Amir et al. (2009), who conducted the study of attention training for people with generalized social phobia discussed in Chapter 3, told readers that

> participants were enrolled in the study serially at two sites, the University of Georgia (UGA, $n = 24$) and San Diego State University (SDSU, $n = 20$), between January 2003 and October 2007. (p. 964)

This study was run over a period of 5 years. Given the nature of the study, this information is likely inconsequential but can be especially important if the data are in some way tied to a particular circumstance, for example, reactions to a natural disaster or political event.

Statistics and Data Analysis

> The description of your statistics and data analysis should include information concerning problems with statistical assumptions and/or data distributions that could affect the validity of findings.

In the Method section, you may have provided a subsection describing your statistical analysis or analysis strategy. Then, in the Results section, you need to describe any problems that may have arisen after you collected your data. These problems might arise because some data points have troubling characteristics or because the data set as a whole does not meet some assumptions of the statistical tests.

What the particular problems might be will vary from data set to data set and statistical test to statistical test. For example, you might find your data contain a statistical outlier, a value so different from the others it is unlikely to be part of the same population of data. Perhaps there was a recording error or perhaps a participant wanted to sabotage your study (heaven forbid!). Or perhaps you want to conduct a particular analysis requiring that certain assumptions be met by the data. If these assumptions are not met, this might lead you to transform your data or choose another analysis. It is critical to your reader's ability to evaluate and replicate your study that he or she know (a) what the data analysis problem was and (b) how you solved it, if you could.

Let's look at a couple of examples. Risen and Gilovich (2008) described a problem with a skewed data distribution in an article titled "Why People Are Reluctant to Tempt Fate," published in the *Journal of Personality and Social Psychology*. One measure they used involved response latencies, or how long it took participants to choose among a set of possible endings for a story they had just read:

> Because the response latencies were skewed, we used natural log transformations in all response time analyses, but we report the raw means for ease of interpretation. (Risen & Gilovich, 2008, p. 296)

Adank, Evans, Stuart-Smith, and Scott (2009), in their study of comprehension of familiar and unfamiliar accents, conducted an analysis looking for statistical outliers:

> All values larger than the average plus 2.5 standard deviations per noise level as calculated across all participants in both groups were considered to be outliers and excluded from analysis. (p. 524)

Here Adank et al. tell us the criterion for identifying a data point as an outlier but not the number of excluded points. Sometimes researchers do not remove outliers but instead reset their value to their next nearest neighbor.

Missing Data

Your description of any missing data problems you encountered should include

- frequency or percentages of missing data;
- empirical evidence and/or theoretical arguments for the causes of data that are missing, for example, missing completely at random (sometimes abbreviated as "MCAR"), missing at random (sometimes abbreviated as "MAR"), or missing not at random (sometimes abbreviated as "MNAR"); and
- methods for addressing missing data, if used.

A problem that arises in many studies is missing data. Data typically are missing because (a) participants do not respond to all of the questions on a questionnaire or refuse to respond to certain questions in interviews, (b) equipment fails, or (c) the study included a follow-up phase and participants could not be located. If this happens, you have some (or even most) of the possible data on these participants but not all of the data.

In these situations, it is important to consider why the data are missing. Little and Rubin (2002) grouped missing data problems into different types. When data are missing completely at random, it means that the reason they are missing has nothing to do with their value or with the value of any other variables in the data analysis. So, in your labeling study, if you lost data from a participant because the computer you were using crashed just before he or she answered some final questions, you can be fairly certain these data were missing completely at random. If data are missing not at random, it means that the reason that they are missing is related to the value. For example, in your labeling study, you might have wanted to see whether participants' suggestibility was related to their ratings of the fragrances (would more suggestible people show more extreme reactions to the Roses and Manure labels?). But if people view being susceptible to influence as a negative personal characteristic, then highly suggestible people might be more inclined to leave blank your question "Are you easily influenced by others?" There are other forms of missing data (e.g., MAR data), but the discussion of these issues quickly becomes complicated.[1]

The important point for us is that if you encountered a missing data problem in your study, the JARS recommends that you describe it and what you did to take it into account when you did your analyses. For example, Norman et al. (2008) described their approach to missing data in their web-based smoking intervention study as follows:

> The influence of missing data was minimized through an assertive tracking approach involving multiple visits to schools after scheduled data collection sessions and working closely with teachers and school administrators who assisted the research team by contacting students in class or sending reminders home. Intensive procedures were used to find students absent at follow-up through collaboration with participating school officials, which resulted in high follow-up rates: 95% at postintervention, 89% at 3-month follow-up, and 87% at 6-month follow-up. The use of multilevel logistic regression models provided alternative strategies to deal with missing data that are comparable to estimation procedures but rely on less data to effectively assess change over time. (p. 804)

It is also possible to impute missing data or to estimate its most likely value given the value of other data you do have. Here is how Fagan, Palkovitz, Roy, and Farrie (2009) handled missing data in their study of nonresident fathers' engagement with their children, in which they needed data from both mothers and fathers to do the desired analyses:

> At Year 1, 19 mothers were not interviewed and 49 had missing data; at Year 3, 29 mothers were not interviewed and 82 had missing data. For those cases in which all mothers' data were missing, the fathers' data were first consulted to

[1]MAR data are like MNAR data, but they can be adjusted for in your analyses.

see whether they reported having any contact with the child. If they did not, zeros were imputed for all mother items. Among mothers who had some missing items, we imputed the respondent's mean for those items that were answered. For the remaining cases, the sample mean for the mother's index was imputed. (p. 1393)

Deleted Cases

For each primary and secondary outcome, you should include a summary of cases deleted from each analysis.

Participants can be deleted from studies because their data contain too many missing values. Sometimes participants can have complete data, but you may decide they should be omitted from the analyses for other reasons. Other reasons might include an indication that the participant did not understand the study's instructions. In experimental studies, researchers often include a *manipulation check* that is meant to gauge whether the manipulated conditions were attended to and believed by the participant. For example, you might ask participants after collecting your labeling data from them whether they remembered the name of the fragrance. If they did not, you might delete the participants. Or you might ask them what they thought of the name. If they said, "Didn't believe it. No one would name a perfume Manure!" you might delete their data.

If you deleted participants, the JARS recommends that your report include (a) the number of participants deleted and (b) an explanation for why each case was tossed out. You should also say whether the deletion criterion was established before the experiment began or adopted post hoc, after the data were collected and a problem was discovered (e.g., include a statement such as "We did not anticipate that participants would find the name Manure implausible, but because some did [*n* = *x*], we excluded these participants from the analyses").

Here is how Amir et al. (2009) described why and how many trials were eliminated from their study of attention training for people with generalized social phobia:

We first eliminated response latencies for inaccurate trials. Inaccurate trials were trials in which the probe was presented on the left side and the participant pressed the button corresponding to the right side, or vice versa. This procedure resulted in the elimination of 1% of the trials. In addition, response latencies less than 50 ms and greater than 1,200 ms were considered outliers and were also eliminated from the analysis. These ranges were determined from the inspection of the data using box plots and resulted in eliminating 1% of the trials. (p. 967)

Thus, these researchers deleted responses (not participants' entire set of data) for two reasons.

Adank et al. (2009) deleted participants' data (not individual responses) from their study of accent comprehension for the same two reasons:

The data of four participants from the SE [standard English] listener group were excluded from further analysis, as they did not perform the task correctly. The data from three GE [Glasgow English] participants were excluded, as more than 20% of their responses were slower than 3.5 s. (p. 523)

Subgroups, Cells, and Null Hypothesis Significance Testing

For each primary and secondary outcome and for each subgroup, you should include a summary of

- subgroup or cell sample sizes, cell means, standard deviations or other estimates of precision, and other descriptive statistics; and
- effect sizes and confidence intervals.

For inferential statistics (null hypothesis significance testing), you should include information about

- the a priori Type I error rate adopted; and
- direction, magnitude, degrees of freedom, and exact p level, even if no significant effect is reported.

The *Publication Manual* (APA, 2010b) provides detailed descriptions of ways to present the sample sizes, cell means, standard deviations, effect sizes, confidence intervals, and the results of any null hypothesis significance tests you may have conducted. Most often, if your study included participants in different conditions (e.g., Roses and Manure labels for a fragrance) and you have several dependent or outcome variables, present the different sample sizes, cell means, and standard deviations in a table. The first half of Chapter 5 in the *Publication Manual* (APA, 2010b, pp. 125–150) describes how to prepare tables. Table 4.1 reproduces the table of results from Vadasy and Sanders's (2008) evaluation of a reading intervention. The table succinctly displays lots of data; it includes the cell means and standard deviations for the major outcome variables, each measured twice, as well as the gain from the first to the second measurement. Because the cell sample sizes were identical for all measures and all times, Vadasy and Sanders reported these two numbers only in the table note (along with the full definitions for all of the abbreviations in the table). Had the cell means varied for different measures or times (perhaps because of missing data), readers would expect to see additional columns with these entered. From this table, it is possible for readers to recalculate many of the inferential statistics in the report and to calculate effect sizes for any two-group comparison. This ensures that the study will be useful for researchers who want to include it in future meta-analyses.

In Chapter 3 of this volume, I introduced the three effect-size metrics that are used most often by psychologists. The JARS recommends that effect sizes and confidence intervals be reported along with the results of any null hypothesis statistical tests you may have conducted, whether or not they are significant. How to report these is covered in the *Publication Manual* (APA, 2010b) as well, especially in Chapter 4, section 4.44, Statistics in Text (pp. 116–117).

From the viewpoint of reporting standards, the critical aspect is that this information needs to be reported completely; include everything recommended in the

Table 4.1. Example of Table With Sample Sizes, Means, and Standard Deviations

Observed Pretests, Posttests, and Pretest–Posttest Gains

Measure	Treatment						Control					
	Pretest		Posttest		Gain		Pretest		Posttest		Gain	
	M	SD	M	SD	M	SD	M	SD	M	SD	M	SD
RAN	87.7	10.12					90.5	9.99				
WR accuracy	94.3	7.63	97.8	7.04	3.5	5.66	96.5	6.09	98.3	6.25	1.8	5.29
WR efficiency	87.9	9.19	94.7	10.12	6.8	7.72	89.2	8.50	94.6	10.49	5.5	8.09
PRF-U	40.0	18.35	83.1	22.27	43.2	16.53	42.3	19.91	79.0	23.76	36.7	19.56
PRF-A	37.5	16.84	68.3	26.38	30.8	18.50	39.6	17.13	62.5	26.63	22.9	18.36
Fluency rate	77.0	8.23	88.6	13.13	11.6	9.62	78.6	8.07	86.8	12.10	8.2	9.25
Comprehension	84.8	13.09	92.8	15.72	8.0	13.74	87.6	13.71	92.9	16.22	5.4	16.12

Note. Treatment group *N* = 82, control group *N* = 80. Norm-referenced standard scores (raw scores adjusted for age) were used for all measures except PRF-U and PRF-A; for these two measures, words correct per minute were used. The control group performed significantly higher on the WR accuracy pretest. RAN = Letter Naming subtest from the Rapid Automatized Naming/Rapid Alternating Stimulus tests; WR accuracy = Word Identification subtest from the Woodcock Reading Mastery Test—Revised/Normative Update; WR efficiency = Sight Word subtest from the Test of Word Reading Efficiency; PRF-U and PRF-A = words-correct-per-minute performance on uniform and alternate passages, respectively, from the Oral Reading Fluency subtest from the Dynamic Indicators of Basic Early Literacy Skills; Fluency rate = Rate subtest from the Gray Oral Reading Tests-4 (GORT); Comprehension = GORT Comprehension subtest. From "Repeated Reading Intervention: Outcomes and Interactions With Readers' Skills and Classroom Instruction," by P. F. Vadasy and E. A. Sanders, 2008, *Journal of Educational Psychology, 100*, p. 280. Copyright 2008 by the American Psychological Association.

JARS. Yes, some of this information will seem redundant. After all, effect sizes can be calculated from sample sizes, means, and standard deviations (Borenstein, 2009), and if related null hypothesis significance testing is significant, the confidence interval for an effect size will indicate this (by not containing zero). Still, you cannot expect readers to calculate these values for themselves, and you do not know which statistic will be of particular interest to different readers of your report. A complete report contains them all. You are also expected to provide a precise p value for each test, up to three decimal places, and to use the "less than" symbol (<) only when the p value is less than .001.

Multivariate Data Analyses

> For multivariable analytic systems (e.g., multivariate analyses of variance, regression analyses, structural equation modeling analyses, and hierarchical linear modeling), also include the associated variance–covariance (or correlation) matrix or matrices.

The JARS recommends that you include the associated variance–covariance or correlation matrix when you are reporting the results of a multivariate analysis. Again, this is important for purposes of replicating your analysis and for secondary uses of your data. For example, O'Neill, Vandenberg, DeJoy, and Wilson (2009) tested latent variable models in their study of anger in the workplace. They presented a table, reproduced here as Table 4.2, that provides the correlation matrix on which these analyses were based. The table also contains the means and standard deviations for each variable.

With this matrix, other researchers will be able to use O'Neill et al.'s (2009) data in many different ways. For example, someone doing a meta-analysis of the relationship between alcohol use and job turnover can find in the matrix the correlation between these two variables ($r = .10$). Their data can contribute to this meta-analysis even though this was not the primary purpose of the study.

Estimation Problems

> You should describe any estimation problems (e.g., failure to converge, bad solution spaces) you encounter as well as any anomalous data points.

Estimation problems typically involve complex data analyses that for one reason or another have gone awry. Let me give you a "simple" example. In the labeling study, you might have decided to use a logistical regression (Menard, 2002) to predict whether participants indicated they would purchase the fragrance. Logistic regressions are used

■ **Table 4.2.** Example of Table With Correlation Matrix

Means, Standard Deviations, and Correlations

Variable	M	SD	1	2	3	4	5
1. Anger	1.80	0.67	.88				
2. POS	3.03	0.90	−.26	.94			
3. High-risk behaviors	0.30	0.24	.10	−.01	—		
4. Accidents	1.80	0.55	.16	−.11	.05	—	
5. Turnover intention	2.01	1.34	.18	−.39	−.01	.10	—
6. Total alcohol	18.06	44.11	.16	−.02	.14	.06	.10
7. Absence	1.76	1.09	.17	−.11	.06	.20	.12
8. Age	3.87	1.72	−.18	.03	.03	−.13	−.13
9. Supervisor/managerial responsibility	0.78	0.44	−.08	.03	.04	−.03	.03
10. Education	3.19	1.17	−.04	−.11	−.12	−.05	.08
11. Tenure	3.48	1.24	.11	−.24	−.02	−.02	.04
12. Gender	0.69	0.46	−.06	−.04	.10	.03	.09
13. White	0.78	0.41	.09	−.02	.04	−.01	−.04
14. Black	0.08	0.27	−.04	.01	−.01	.01	.01
15. Hispanic	0.06	0.24	−.06	.01	−.05	.01	.01
16. Inventory loss	4,391,430.00	611,504.00	.48[a]	−.86[a]			
17. Unit turnover	0.30	0.09	.52[a]	−.39[a]			
18. High involvement	3.30	0.87	−.21	.63	−.01	−.09	−.36

Note. Internal consistency values are in italics. Any correlation in Rows 1 through 15 ($n = 1,136$) with an absolute value of .05 or greater is statistically significant at $p < .05$. The correlations in Rows 16 through 18 ($n = 21$) are statistically siginficant at $p < .05$. Inventory loss and unit turnover were unit-level measures and thus do not have correlations with the variables measured at the individual level. POS = perceived organizational support. Adapted from "Exploring Relationships Among Anger, Perceived Organizational Support, and Workplace Outcomes," by O. A. O'Neill, R. J. Vandenberg, D. M. DeJoy, and M. G. Wilson, 2009, *Journal of Occupational Health Psychology, 14,* p. 326. Copyright 2009 by the American Psychological Association.
[a]These correlations represent the relationships of the between-level index of anger and POS with the inventory loss and turnover variables. The other correlations in this column are between the pooled within-group index of anger and POS (individual level controlling for store-level variation) and the stated variables.

when the outcome (predicted) variable either is dichotomous or has values that range from 0 to 1, representing probability values or proportions. For each participant, the prediction equation results in a value between 0 and 1 that represents the probability that he or she will buy the fragrance. Each predictor variable has a beta weight (and significance level) associated with it. In your logistic regression, the outcome variable takes on only two values (buy or not buy), and you might use as predictors of buying

6	7	8	9	10	11	12	13	14	15	16	17	18
—												
.10	—											
−.07	−.14	—										
−.06	.05	.05	—									
−.04	−.07	.13	.05	—								
.01	−.01	.25	−.30	−.01	—							
.10	−.06	.03	−.06	.10	−.01	—						
.04	−.01	.08	−.01	.04	.05	.01	—					
−.04	−.02	−.06	−.02	−.01	−.05	−.04	−.58	—				
−.02	.03	−.09	.05	−.01	−.03	.02	−.48	−.08	—			
										—		
										.56	—	
−.08	−.05	−.02	.01	−.12	−.30	−.07	−.09	.09	.02	—	—	.93

intention the participants' experimental condition (roses vs. manure), sex, degree of suggestibility, and socioeconomic status.

Your logistic regression program will use an algorithm to calculate the maximum likelihood solution for the prediction equations. It will do this through an iterative process until the iterations converge on a single answer. The convergence may never be perfect, however, and your statistical program has a specified tolerance value that, when reached, stops the iterations and presents that result as the best answer. Sometimes the tolerance value is not reached, and the iterations will go on and on. Rather than do this, the computer will stop after a certain number of iterations and tell you there has been a "failure to converge." In such a case, you will need to (a) reexamine your data to see if there is an identifiable problem that you can address, (b) reset your tolerance level (if allowed), (c) choose from other procedures that alter the algorithm, or (d) abandon the analysis. Whichever option you choose, the JARS recommends that you fully report the problem you encountered and your solution for it.

Statistical Software

> You should describe any statistical software program, if specialized procedures were used.

It is not necessary to tell readers which statistical software program you used to conduct uncomplicated and frequently used statistical tests, for example, *t* tests, analyses of variance, or multiple regressions. However, identifying the program can be important for more sophisticated and complex analyses. Different programs have different features and options, and you need to tell readers which of these you chose. On occasion, these programs vary significantly in the way they conduct complex analyses, which can lead to varied solutions and conclusions.

For example, O'Neill et al. (2009) reported using the Mplus program to conduct latent variable analyses in their study of anger in the workplace:

> We used the Mplus latent variables program (Muthén & Muthén, 2006). Mplus easily permits the control of systematic sources of between-unit variance in testing models where the primary focus is on individual differences. (p. 325)

Note the reference to the *Mplus User's Guide* (Muthén & Muthén, 2006), which contains information on the approach the program uses to solve the equations needed to conduct latent variable analysis.

To reiterate a point I made in Chapter 3, software is also used to control the introduction of stimuli and the collection of data. These are often very specialized programs, and their details should be reported.

Other and Ancillary Analyses

> Report any other analyses performed, including
>
> - adjusted analyses, indicating those that were prespecified and those that were exploratory (although not necessarily in level of detail of primary analyses), and
> - discussion of implications of ancillary analyses for statistical error rates.

Adjusted analyses occur because of problems with the data, like those described earlier, but sometimes the analyses rather than the data are adjusted. For example, Taylor and James (2009), in their study of markers for substance dependence, adjusted the degrees of freedom in their analysis of electrodermal response modulation (ERM) scores rather than the scores themselves:

As expected, ERM scores for the alcohol-dependence-only, illicit-drug-dependence-only, and combined alcohol/illicit-drug-dependence groups were significantly lower than for the control group, $t(30.234) = 1.961$, $p < .029$ (the degree of freedom was adjusted because of unequal variances between groups); $t(117) = 3.036$, $p = .002$; and $t(121) = 2.176$, $p = .016$, respectively. (p. 496)

Vinnars, Thormählen, Gallop, Norén, and Barber (2009) adjusted effect sizes because they wanted their estimate of the impact of supportive–expressive psychotherapy on personality not to reflect changes in symptoms:

Because we were interested in the question of the degree of change in personality and dynamic variables over and beyond the change in symptoms, we also calculated effect sizes adjusted for improvement in SCL-90 [Symptom Checklist–90] for all variables. (p. 368)

I discussed in Chapter 2 the reasons why it is important to designate your hypotheses as either of primary or of secondary interest. The ancillary analyses that you conduct will relate to your secondary hypotheses, or even to analyses for which you have no hypotheses. The more clearly these analyses are labeled *ancillary, exploratory,* or *secondary,* the less they will interfere with the interpretation of the study's main findings. The JARS recommends that you discuss the implications of ancillary analyses for statistical error rates. It is important for you to talk about how you might have adjusted your significance levels in null hypothesis significance testing to take into account the fact that multiple tests could lead to inflated experiment-wise error rates. For example, in your labeling study, if you looked at whether participant sex, socioeconomic status, the time of day the experiment was run, the weather, and the phase of the moon (just to highlight how exploratory some analyses can be!) were related to fragrance ratings, it would be good to clearly label these analyses as ancillary (related to exploratory hypotheses; does the fragrance labeled Manure smell better when the moon is full?) and to adjust (downward) the p level the test result must reach before you will interpret the result as worthy of future attention, perhaps as a primary hypothesis in subsequent studies.

Studies With an Experimental Manipulation or Intervention

Your report should describe the numbers of participants as they moved through the study, including

- total number of groups (if an intervention was administered at the group level) and the number of participants assigned to each group (number of participants who did not complete the experiment or crossed over to other conditions, and explain why, and number of participants used in primary analyses); and
- flow of participants through each stage of the study (see Figure 4.1).

Participant flow. The JARS also recommends how the results of studies that used experimental manipulations should be reported. The first set of recommendations again involves the flowchart of the number of participants progressing through the study. The example diagram presented in Figure 4.1 involves an experimental study, so I covered most of the pertinent issues earlier. The only new issue introduced here is that the JARS recommends that participants who cross over from one condition to another should be accounted for in your description. Crossover occurs when a participant starts in one condition but ends up in another condition.

> Your report should describe evidence on whether the treatment was delivered as intended.

Treatment fidelity. Treatment fidelity relates to the degree to which a treatment is delivered to participants in the manner in which it was intended. The term *treatment fidelity* is used most often in the context of evaluations of experimental treatments or interventions. After all, if the researchers cannot demonstrate that the intervention was implemented as intended, how can we know whether the evaluation is a fair test of its effectiveness? For example, Vadasy and Sanders (2008) reported the results of an evaluation of a reading intervention. Here is how they described what they did to ensure that the intervention was delivered as intended:

> The tutors practiced the protocols during training and received immediate feedback. Following this training, coaches visited tutors biweekly to provide follow-up training and modeling and to collect data on protocol fidelity. . . .
> **Tutor observations.** To monitor treatment implementation fidelity, we collected data via observation forms on (a) tutor adherence to scripted *Quick Reads* protocols, (b) tutor instructional behaviors, and (c) student progress in terms of the amount of time spent actively engaged in reading passages. Tutors' fidelity to protocols was measured using a 5-point rating scale of 1 (*never*) to 5 (*always*) for each intervention step previously described. . . . Prior to onsite tutor observations, we established interobserver reliability among the five researcher–observers using five videotaped *Quick Reads* sessions. (pp. 276–277)

However, treatment fidelity is not the exclusive province of applied research and intervention evaluations. Laboratory experiments also gauge treatment fidelity, but in these cases, it is typically referred to as a *manipulation check*. Thus, Risen and Gilovich (2008), in their study of people's desire not to tempt fate, explained their manipulation check as follows:

> In addition, participants were given a manipulation check to ensure that they had paid attention to the stories. The manipulation check consisted of one recall question for each of the stories. For the umbrella story, participants were asked, "Did Julie bring her umbrella when she packed for school?" Participants were then thanked and debriefed. (p. 299)

Earlier, I discussed manipulation checks in the context of deleting data. Typically, in laboratory contexts, experimental manipulations are pilot tested to ensure they will have the intended impact on most participants. Therefore, it is rare to find a manipulation check in a published article that indicates the manipulation failed. Imagine having to write of your labeling study, "No one in the manure condition believed the manipulation, but here are the results of our study anyway"! Instead, manipulation checks are used to discard the data of those few participants who did not attend to the manipulation or misunderstood it.

> Your report should describe baseline demographics and clinical characteristics of each group.

Baseline data. Table 4.3 displays both the baseline demographics and the clinical characteristics of participants in Amir et al.'s (2009) study of attention training for people with generalized social phobia. Note that it does so for each of the experimental groups separately. Table 4.1, from Vadasy and Sanders's (2008) evaluation of a reading intervention, presents the baseline data for the outcome as pretests along with the posttest

Table 4.3. Example of Table With Both Demographic and Clinical Baseline Characteristics of Participants in More Than One Group

Patient Demographics and Clinical Characteristics

Variable	AMP	ACC
Gender (% women)	63.6	54.5
Age (years)	27.6 (8.3)	31.1 (13.2)
Education (years)	15.4 (2.6)	15.2 (1.9)
Ethnicity (%)		
European American	63.6	81.8
Asian American	13.6	0
African American	9.1	0
Latin American	9.1	13.6
Other	4.5	4.5
Comorbid diagnoses (%)		
Any	50.0	40.9
Generalized anxiety disorder	22.7	13.6
Specific phobia	13.6	4.5
Past treatment for social phobia (%)	50.0	45.5

Note. Standard deviations in parentheses. AMP = attention modification program; ACC = attention control program. From "Attention Training in Individuals With Generalized Social Phobia: A Randomized Controlled Trial," by N. Amir, C. Beard, C. T. Taylor, H. Klumpp, J. Elias, M. Burns, and X. Chen, 2009, *Journal of Consulting and Clinical Psychology, 77,* p. 964. Copyright 2009 by the American Psychological Association.

and gain scores. In this article, the authors presented the demographic characteristics of participants (their grade, age, minority status, etc.) in a separate table.

> Your report should describe whether the analysis was conducted in intent-to-treat, complier average causal effect, other, or multiple ways.

Intent-to-treat analysis. Another problem you can have with your study that needs to be addressed in your report involves noncompliance among participants in a treatment condition. So, for example, in Vinnars et al.'s (2009) evaluation (of the supportive–expressive therapy for people with personality disorders), the therapy was manualized, and participants attended therapy over the course of 1 calendar year. In Amir et al.'s (2009) study (of attention training for people with generalized social phobia), the training protocol involved eight 20-min training sessions delivered over a 4-week period.

What if participants did not attend enough sessions to allow the researchers to feel confident that participants received the treatment as intended? There are several approaches to data analysis, and which one is used can have critical implications for how the results can be interpreted. This is why the JARS recommends that compliance be carefully reported.

First, you can do an intent-to-treat analysis. In this case, all participants are included in the analysis no matter how well their treatment conformed to the treatment protocol. This is what Vinnars et al. (2009) decided to do:

> Using an intent-to-treat approach, all patients were included in the statistical analyses regardless of whether or not they completed treatment. (p. 368)

When an intent-to-treat analysis is conducted, it means that the random assignment of participants to conditions remains, but the resulting treatment effects may or may not reflect the impact of the treatment. You might say that your statistical tests relate to the causal effect of being assigned to the treatment condition and to whatever exposure to the treatment this assignment results in. That is not the same as the causal effect of the treatment itself.

Alternatively, you can decide to exclude those participants you feel have not complied. In this approach, you have confidence that the participants in your analysis have experienced the treatment as you intended. However, if many participants were omitted from the analysis because of noncompliance, we again confront the possibility that they were different from participants in the control group before the experiment began, and thus random assignment is compromised. This is what Amir et al. (2009) did:

> Analyses were conducted on treatment completers (AMP [attention modification program], $n = 22$; ACC [attention control condition], $n = 22$). We chose this approach rather than an intention-to-treat analysis given the differential dropout rate between the AMP group ($n = 0$) and ACC group ($n = 4$). However, intent-to-treat analyses did not differ from the analyses reported on treatment completers only. (p. 966)

Note that for Amir et al., noncompliers were dropouts, not people the researchers decided had not received the treatment as intended. This makes clear the relationship between complier-only analyses and the ability to draw strong causal inferences about the effectiveness of the treatment. It should also be clear why the JARS calls for you to report which type of analysis you conducted.[2]

> Your report should describe all important adverse events or side effects in each intervention group.

Adverse side effects. Needless to say, if you conduct an experiment, typically an evaluation of a treatment or an intervention, and discover that it had harmful or undesirable side effects on participants, you are obligated to disclose these in your research report and note how frequently they occurred. What constitutes an adverse side effect is a complex matter that I cannot go into here, but it is important if you are exploring the effectiveness of a new treatment that you be aware of its potential to have both helpful and harmful effects.[3]

When you request permission from your institutional review board to conduct your study, you will be asked to consider and discuss both positive and negative effects and what you will do to minimize the latter. This will require you to expand your thinking about how participants will react to your treatment or intervention. Should any of these undesirable effects actually occur, your readers need to know about it.

Statistical Methods

> For studies using random assignment, you should describe
>
> - statistical methods used to compare groups on primary outcome(s);
> - statistical methods used for additional analyses, such as subgroup analyses and adjusted analyses; and
> - statistical methods used for mediation analyses.
>
>   For studies using nonrandom assignment, you should describe
>
> - statistical methods used to compare study groups on primary outcomes(s), including complex methods for correlated data;
> - statistical methods used for additional analyses, such as subgroup analyses and adjusted analyses (e.g., methods for modeling pretest differences and adjusting for them); and
> - statistical methods used for mediation analyses.

---

[2]Complier average causal effect, mentioned in the box on page 70, is a statistical technique for estimating the causal effect of a treatment (not treatment assignment) when noncompliance is a problem (see Little, Long, & Lin, 2009).
[3]If you are testing fragrance labels for a perfume company and several participants in the manure condition pass out, readers need to know!

Most of the items that the JARS recommends you cover when reporting a study with an experimental manipulation are straightforward or have already been covered earlier in this chapter. Again, the JARS recommends that you be as comprehensive and as transparent about the reporting of statistics as you have been about your rationale for doing the study and your method in carrying it out.

Now, with all of the details laid out, you turn to the task of pulling it all together and drawing the substantive inferences about what you found.

5

Describing What Your Results Mean: The Discussion Section

Now that you have provided your readers with a thorough rendering of the mechanics of your study and the results of your statistical analyses, it is time to tell them what you think it all means. The Journal Article Reporting Standards (JARS) recommends including several important elements. First, you must summarize what you found by telling readers which results were most essential and which were secondary. You do not need to label them in this way (e.g., by having subsections called Primary Findings and Secondary Findings), although it would be okay to do so. You make the importance of your different results clear by when, how, and in what depth you choose to discuss them. In your labeling study, if your interest was primarily theoretical, you might spend considerable time detailing and interpreting what you found on the measures related to the fragrance's pleasantness, but you might mention only briefly how the label affected buying intentions. If you had more applied motives for doing the study, the two types of measures might get equal attention. Some secondary findings (reported in the Results section) might hardly be mentioned, however compelled you may feel to explain everything.

Also, in the Discussion section you interpret your findings in light of the issues that motivated you to do the study in the first place, as described in your introduction. State how you think your study advances knowledge on these issues. For example, in the fragrance labeling study, what do you know about labeling effects that you did not know before? If you cannot answer this question, your study may not be of great interest to others.

Finally, cast an evaluative eye on your own work, taking a step back and looking at both its strengths and weaknesses. This permits you to propose the next steps that will advance the field.

It is typical for the Discussion section to begin with a recap of the rationale for the study. You should be able to return to the introduction, find the sentences you wrote there, and rephrase these at the beginning of the Discussion section. For example, O'Neill, Vandenberg, DeJoy, and Wilson (2009) began their Discussion section with two simple sentences meant to remind readers of the broad agenda that motivated their research:

> The goal of the current study was to extend organizational support theory through an examination of anger in the workplace. We first examined whether anger was an antecedent or a consequence of employees' perceptions of conditions or events in the workplace. (p. 330)

Adank, Evans, Stuart-Smith, and Scott (2009) did the same:

> The purpose of the present study was to determine the relative processing cost of comprehending speech in an unfamiliar native accent under adverse listening conditions. As this processing cost could not always be reliably estimated in quiet listening conditions . . . , we investigated the interaction between adverse listening conditions and sentences in an unfamiliar native accent in two experiments. (p. 527)

A quick summary serves as a simple reminder of your purpose. After the detailed Method and Results sections, it is good to draw your readers' attention back to the big issues. That said, you should realize that readers will have different levels of interest in your article and will read different sections with different levels of care and attention. Do not feel insulted if I suggest some readers will skip the Method and Results sections entirely (after you worked on them so hard!) or just skim them quickly and move directly from reading your introduction to reading your Discussion section. For these readers, the brief summary at the beginning of the Discussion section will sound a lot like what they read at the end of your introduction. That is okay. If you consider that different readers will read different chunks of your article, it makes sense to help keep them all on track.

Statement About the Primary Hypotheses

> Your discussion should include a statement of support or nonsupport for all original hypotheses
>
> - distinguished by primary and secondary hypotheses and
> - post hoc explanations.
>
> It should also delineate similarities and differences between your results and the work of others.

After the restatement of the goals for your research, the JARS recommends that you provide a summary statement of your principal findings. Not every finding should be included, just the ones that support or refute your major hypotheses. These findings should be the focus of the discussion that follows. You can return to findings that help you explain your principal findings or that are of secondary interest later in the Discussion section. For example, O'Neill et al. (2009) immediately followed their two-sentence restatement of goals with a two-sentence recap of what they considered to be their major finding:

> Although a negative reciprocal relationship between anger and POS [perceived organizational support] was hypothesized, only the negative relationship from POS to anger was supported. The relationship of POS and anger lends support to the social exchange perspective; anger seems to result from employees' negative perceptions of workplace conditions rather than anger serving as a filter for negative perceptions of the organization, as suggested by affect-as-information and mood congruency theories. (p. 330)

Note that O'Neill et al. pointed out that they had hypothesized a reciprocal relationship but did not find it. They also said that their finding supported one theoretical interpretation of the data but not two others. This is a perfect way to set up the more detailed discussion that follows.

Fagan, Palkovitz, Roy, and Farrie (2009) were also relatively brief in summing up their findings:

> The findings of this study are consistent with our hypothesis suggesting that risk and resilience factors of low-income, urban fathers who are unmarried and not residing with the mother and baby at birth, later nonresidence with the child, and mother–father relationship quality are significant components of an ecological model of paternal engagement with young children. (pp. 1398–1399)

This simple categorical statement of support is then followed by three pages of summary and interpretation of the findings.

Risen and Gilovich (2008) also began with a succinct summary of their findings:

> Despite explicit knowledge that tempting fate does not change the likelihood of a broad range of negative outcomes, participants gave responses that reflected the intuitive belief that it does. Thus, even if they rationally recognized that there is no mechanism to make rain more likely when they leave behind an umbrella . . . participants reported that they thought these particular negative outcomes were indeed more likely following such actions. (p. 303)

However, two sentences is not the limit for how long the summary should be. Goldinger, He, and Papesh (2009) went into a bit more detail about their findings regarding other-race bias (ORB) in their opening summation:

> Having observed the ORB in recognition, we, as our primary goal, sought to examine information-gathering behavior during learning. Considering first eye movements, widespread differences emerged between own- and cross-race face processing. In quantitative terms, when participants studied own-race faces, their eye fixations were brief and plentiful. Relative to cross-race trials, own-race trials elicited more fixations to facial features, briefer gaze times per fixation, more fixations to unique features, and fewer regressions. All these findings were reflected in an index of total distance traveled by the eyes during encoding, which we used for most analyses. The differences in eye movements were not an artifact of

recognition accuracy: The same patterns were observed in subsets of learning trials leading only to eventual hits. In qualitative terms, participants favored different features across races (see Figures 2 and 8). (p. 1120)

Goldinger et al. (2009) chose to mention each of their primary measures in the summary, whereas authors of the earlier examples chose more general statements of support and nonsupport. Which approach you take should be determined by how consistent findings are across measures (can you quickly mention them in groups or will you lose readers in the details?) and how much attention you intend to pay to each outcome measure separately.

These four examples present the happy news that the authors' primary hypotheses largely were confirmed by the data. But the opening summary is not always a bed of roses; sometimes the manure is evident. Evers, Brouwers, and Tomic (2006) had to contend with a deeper level of nonsupport for their primary hypotheses. First, though, they also began with a brief restatement of purpose and research design:

> In the present article, we examined the question of whether management coaching might be effective. To this end, we conducted a quasi-experiment in which we compared an experimental group of managers with a control group at Time 1 and Time 2. We measured hypothesized outcome expectations and self-efficacy beliefs on three domains of behavior, for example, acting in a balanced way, setting one's own goals, and mindful living and working. (p. 179)

However, things did not turn out exactly as they had hoped:

> We found a significant difference between the experimental and the control group on only outcome expectations and not on self-efficacy beliefs regarding the domain "acting in a balanced way." (Evers et al., 2006, p. 179)

Thus, Evers et al. did not get exactly the results they had expected. Still, they provided a reasonable post hoc explanation for why this might have been the case; the intervention simply did not have time to effect all the changes they had expected:

> These objectives clearly show that improving existing skills and developing new ones precede new beliefs, convictions, and judgments, which may explain the nonsignificance of differences between the experimental and the control groups with respect to the variable "to act in a balanced way." In the short time between measuring the variable at Time 1 and Time 2, self-efficacy beliefs with respect to "acting in a balanced way" may not have developed yet. It may also be that managers have come to the conviction that some specific type of behavior will be advantageous but that they still experience some inner feelings of resistance toward getting rid of their old behavior. (Evers et al., 2006, p. 180)

Adank et al. (2009) delved a bit deeper into the nuances of their listening comprehension findings and the relationship of these findings to past research. Of their primary hypotheses, they wrote the following:

> The results for the GE [Glasgow English] listener group in Experiment 1 showed that they made an equal number of errors and responded equally fast for both

accents. The finding that the performance of the GE listeners was not affected by the accent of the speaker confirms that the processing delay for the GE sentences by the SE [Standard English] listener group was due to the relative unfamiliarity of the SE listeners with the Glaswegian accent. SE listeners thus benefited from their relative familiarity with SE. (Adank et al., 2009, p. 527)

In summary, your Discussion section should commence with a restatement of your goals and a summary of your findings that relate to those goals. You do not have to list every finding. However, the JARS recommends that you present a complete picture of the findings that relate to your primary hypotheses, regardless of whether they were supportive. If you found unsupportive results, try to explain why.

Comparisons With the Work of Others

Adank et al. (2009) highlighted the importance of an interaction between listening comprehension and amount of background noise. This led them directly into a discussion of how their work compares with the work of others:

> No effects were found for processing the unfamiliar native accent in quiet. This result shows again that the cognitive processing cost cannot easily be estimated in quiet conditions (cf. Floccia et al., 2006). However, in both experiments, an interaction was found between the unfamiliar accent and moderately poor SNRs [signal-to-noise ratios] . . . listeners slow down considerably for these SNRs for the unfamiliar accent. A similar interaction has been found in experiments comparing the processing speed for synthetic versus natural speech (e.g., Pisoni et al., 1985). In conclusion, it seems justified to assume that processing an unfamiliar native accent in noise is delayed compared with processing a familiar native accent in noise. (Adank et al., 2009, p. 527)

Note that Adank et al. (2009) compared their results with the work of others in two different ways, both of which were consistent with their findings. Their first reference to another study is used to suggest that others' research confirms their finding. Essentially, Adank et al. replicated this earlier result. The second reference to another study also suggests a replication, but here the earlier study varied from their study in an important way in that it compared processing speed between natural and synthetic speech rather than two accents of the same language.

Of course, your comparison with past research will not always indicate congruency between your results and the interpretations of other studies. Indeed, you might have undertaken your study to demonstrate that a past finding was fallacious or cannot be obtained under certain circumstances. Adank et al. (2009) pointed out an inconsistency of the former type between their results and past findings:

> On the basis of Evans and Iverson's results, one could hypothesize that familiarity with a native accent does not come from being exposed to it through the media alone but that interaction with speakers of that accent (or even adapting one's own speech to that accent) is also required. However, our results do not provide support for this hypothesis, as GE listeners were equally fast for GE and SE.

> The GE listeners had been born and raised in Glasgow, and although they were highly familiar with SE through the media, they had had little experience of interacting with SE speakers on a regular basis. (p. 527)

Risen and Gilovich (2008) also pointed out how their findings contradicted some explanations for superstitious behavior:

> Although most traditional accounts of superstition maintain that such beliefs exist because people lack certain cognitive capacities (Frazer, 1922; Levy-Bruhl, 1926; Piaget, 1929; Tylor, 1873), the work presented here adds to accumulating evidence of magical thinking on the part of people who, according to traditional accounts, should not hold such beliefs. (p. 303)

In summary, the JARS recommends that you place your work in the context of earlier work. You can cite work that your study replicates and extends, but you should also include work with results or predictions at odds with your own. In this regard, if your labeling study showed that when the fragrance was labeled Roses it was rated more pleasant than when labeled Manure, it would be perfectly appropriate for you to point out that this finding was in conflict with the assertion by Juliet Capulet.[1] When you do this, you should propose reasons why the contradictions may have occurred.

Interpretation of Results

Your interpretation of the results should take into account

- sources of potential bias and other threats to internal validity,
- imprecision of measures,
- overall number of tests or overlap among tests, and
- other limitations or weakness of the study.

The JARS focuses its prescription for what to include in the interpretation of results on aspects of the research design and analyses that limit your ability to draw confident conclusions from your study. This is not because your Discussion section should focus only on the study's limitations but because you may be tempted to disregard these and to promote your research by discussing only its strengths. Typically, this strategy does not work. Your manuscript will get a careful reading once it has been submitted for peer review. If you do not point out your study's weaknesses, the peer reviewers will. Those who will read your work know every study has flaws; it is impossible to conduct a flawless study. By being transparent about what you know was not perfect, you convey to the reader a scientific posture that puts your article in a better light. By turning a critical eye on your own work, you instill confidence in your readers that you know what you are doing.

---

[1]Sorry, Juliet (see Collins, 1977; Kohli, Harich, & Leuthesser, 2005).

Strengths of the Study

That said, even though the JARS focuses on weaknesses, do not forget to point out your study's strengths. For example, Taylor and James (2009) began their discussion of biomarkers for substance dependence (SD) with a positive assertion about their findings:

> SD is a common and costly disorder, and efforts to uncover its etiology are under way on several fronts. . . . Other work has shown promise for ERM [electrodermal response modulation] as an independent marker for SD, and the present study provides initial evidence of the possible specificity of ERM as a putative biomarker for SD. This could enhance the search for underlying genetic factors and neural pathways that are associated not with externalizing disorders generally but with SD more specifically. (p. 496)

Moller, Forbes-Jones, and Hightower (2008), who studied the effects of the age composition of classrooms on preschoolers' cognitive, motor, and social skills, began their General Discussion section with a strong statement of what was best about their work:

> This investigation represents a unique and important contribution to the literature on preschool classroom age composition in a number of respects. First, the study included a sample far larger than that in any previously conducted research. . . . Second, this research is among the first to use a well-validated assessment of early childhood development (i.e., the COR [Child Observation Record]) in a variety of domains (social, motor, and cognitive) and to include assessments at two time points (spaced approximately 6 months apart). (p. 748)

So, "This study was the first . . . the biggest . . . the best" are all good ways to think about your study's strengths. But neither Taylor and James (2009) nor Moller et al. (2008) stopped there. They also described some of the less positive aspects of their work.

Limitations or Weaknesses of the Study

If your study drew its inspiration from theories or problems that posited causal relationships among variables but your research design had some limitations in allowing such inferences, the JARS recommends that this be acknowledged. For example, Moller et al. (2008) included the following acknowledgment in their discussion:

> Another limitation of this research involves the correlational nature of these data. Empirical investigations that manipulate the age composition of preschool classrooms, with random assignment to condition, are warranted. (p. 750)

Fagan et al. (2009) put this same concern about internal validity in proximity to their strongest interpretation of their study:

> Our findings suggest that as time passes, risk and resilience factors continue to play a significant role in relation to paternal engagement. Furthermore, our

findings reveal that the patterns of interrelatedness between risk, resilience, and engagement (direct and mediating effects) are the same when the child is 3 years old as they are when the child is 1. Although causal relationships cannot be inferred from our analyses, our approach to measuring risk and resilience in fathers is an improvement to previous research. (p. 1399)

O'Neill et al. (2009) acknowledged a similar weakness in internal validity that was due to their research design:

The design of the study precludes drawing causal inferences at the individual level of analysis. Hence, a stronger test of these relationships is needed, particularly in light of potential reciprocity between POS and anger. (p. 330)

If your research design did not allow for strong causal inferences, it is also critical that you avoid the use of causal language in the interpretation of your results. For example, if you correlated the positivity of people's reactions to perfume names with their evaluation of the fragrance itself, avoid using terms such as *caused, produced,* or *affected* that suggest your study uncovered a causal connection between labels and fragrance evaluations. It is easy to slip up on this matter because we all use causal language in everyday conversation without being consciously aware of doing so.

In addition to their caution about internal validity, O'Neill et al. (2009) alerted their readers to some concerns about their measurements:

A final limitation is that our anger measure did not capture feelings of anger specifically directed toward the organization or its members. In this way, our conceptual model is not perfectly aligned with the operational definitions of the variables. (p. 331)

Generalizability

Your report should discuss the generalizability (external validity) of the findings, taking into account

- the target population and
- other contextual issues.

The JARS addresses limitations related to internal validity, measurement, and statistics in one section. It gives a separate treatment to concerns about the generalization of findings. Evaluating the generalizability of your study's findings involves you in at least four different assessments.

First, you need to consider the people or other units involved in the study in comparison with the larger target population they are meant to represent. I discussed the importance of circumscribing these boundaries in Chapter 3. Now it is time to address the issue head on and attempt to answer the questions I set out: Are the people in the study in some way a restricted subsample of the target population? If they are, do the restrictions suggest that the results pertain to some but not all members of the target population?

Second, generalization across people is only one domain you must consider. As noted in the JARS, other contextual variations should be considered. If your study involved an experimental manipulation, you need to ask how the way the manipulation was operationalized in your study might be different from how it would be experienced in a natural setting. A third assessment involves considering whether the outcome variables you used in your study are a good representation of all the outcomes that might be of interest. For example, if you measured only participants' preference for a fragrance, does this preference generalize to buying intentions? Finally, was there something unique about the settings of your study that suggests similar results might not be obtained in other settings? Could being in a psychology lab while choosing between two fragrances with different labels lead to a greater focus on the fragrance name than would making the same choice while standing at a perfume counter with dozens of fragrances in a large department store?

Our example studies provide instances in which the researchers grappled with each of these types of generalizations. Taylor and James (2009) provided the following cautions regarding the generalization of their findings across people:

> Although the present study holds promise in helping move research into biological factors associated with SD forward, it had limitations that warrant mention. First, the PD [personality disorder]-only group was difficult to fill given the high comorbidity of PD with SD, and the results for that relatively small group should not be overinterpreted. Second, the sample comprised college students, and it is possible that a clinical sample with more extreme presentations of PD and SD could produce different results. (p. 497)

Here, Taylor and James (2009) expressed two concerns about generalization across people. First, they wanted readers to know that people with PD but without SD were rare—the sample was small, so be careful in drawing conclusions about them. Second, they pointed out that the study used only college students, so even the people who were identified as having SD and/or PD were probably less extreme on these characteristics than were people seeking clinical treatment, and thus making generalizations to more extreme populations should be done with caution.

Amir et al. (2009) addressed the issues of generalization of their attention-training intervention to combat social phobia across people and settings:

> The finding that similar treatment outcomes were obtained within the current study at separate sites with differing demographic profiles, as well as in an independent laboratory . . . , supports the generalizability of the attention modification program across settings. (p. 969)

However, the stimuli used in their attention training also led them to appraise the generalizability of results:

> Although the training stimuli used in the current study included faces conveying signs of disgust, there is evidence to suggest that disgust-relevant stimuli activate brain regions also implicated in the processing of other emotional stimuli such as fear. (Amir et al., 2009, p. 969)

Even Killeen, Sanabria, and Dolgov (2009), whose study focused on as basic a process as response conditioning and extinction and used pigeons as subjects, had to grapple with the issue of generalization, in this case across behaviors:

> A limitation of the current analysis is its focus on one well-prepared response, appetitive key pecking in the pigeon. The relative importance of operant and respondent control will vary substantially depending on the response system studied. (p. 467)

As a final example, Fagan et al. (2009) pointed out a limitation of their study related to generalization across time:

> Although the . . . data provide one of the most comprehensive views of this population over time, the operationalized measures provide snapshots of fathers at the time of measurement, and we are attempting to understand the processes and development of father–child relationships across time. (p. 1403)

The overall message to be taken from my discussion of the JARS recommendations about treatment of the limitations of your study is that you should not be afraid to state what these limitations are. Here, I have only sampled from the example studies; there were many more mentions of flaws and limits I did not reproduce. Still, all of these studies got published in top journals in their field. Again, adopting a critical posture toward your own work speaks well of you and instills confidence in readers that you understood what you were doing. The advancement of knowledge was your first priority.

Implications

> Your article should discuss implications for future research, practice, and/or policy.

Your final task in the Discussion section involves detailing what you think are the implications of your findings for theory, practice, policy, and/or future research. Which of these areas is emphasized most depends on the purposes of your study. However, it is not impossible that all four will deserve mention. For example, Moller et al. (2008) included a Theoretical Implications subsection in their Discussion section:

> The findings from the present investigation strongly support the theory-based predictions offered by Piaget (1932) and others, who argued that interacting with peers who are close in age and ability will result in optimal learning. At the same time, these findings are not entirely inconsistent with predictions offered by Vygotsky (1930/1978) and others, who argued for mixed-age interaction principally on the basis of the merits implicit for younger children in these contexts. (p. 749)

Moller et al. (2008) were equally if not more interested in the practical implications of their work. They began their discussion by stating the strong message of their study for how classroom age grouping should be carried out:

> We consistently observed a significant main effect at the classroom level for classroom age composition, which suggested that a wide range in children's ages within a classroom (and high standard deviations in terms of age) was negatively related to development. . . . In this context, the present research strongly suggests that reconsideration of the issue of classroom age composition in early childhood education is warranted. (Moller et al., 2008, p. 749)

O'Neill et al. (2009) thought their findings had an important lesson for organizations' policies and practices:

> The good news is that if an organization successfully influences employees' perceived organizational support, anger, withdrawal behaviors, accidents, and high-risk behaviors will decline. Anger reduction is particularly important for the organization, as highlighted by the costs in terms of employee turnover and loss of inventory. (p. 331)

Future Research

Researchers often joke that concluding a study with the call for more research is a requirement, lest the public lose sight of the value of their enterprise and the need to keep researchers employed. In fact, a study that solves a problem, whether theoretical or practical, once and for all is a rare occurrence indeed. The call for new research is always justified, and now you can cite the JARS as giving you license to do so.

The limitations of a study will lead to suggestions for new research with improvements in design. So Moller et al. (2008) called for future experimental research, as noted earlier, because their study on classroom age grouping was correlational in design. Or the results of the study will suggest new questions that need answering. For example, Fagan et al. (2009) stated the agenda for future research in the form of questions in a subsection titled Future Research:

> The study raises questions regarding the importance of early adaptations of fathers during the transition to fatherhood. Why do some men experience impending fatherhood as a wake-up call to improve their lives by reducing risk and increasing developmental resources, whereas others seem to eschew the development of personal resources that would position them to be more engaged fathers? What are the specific meanings of fathering for men in challenging circumstances, and what are the processes and conditions that allow some men to make positive adjustments to their lives and become involved fathers? What is the role of birth mothers in facilitating and discouraging men's transitions within fathering? Are there interventions or policies that would increase the proportion of men who reduce risk and increase resilience during various transitions within fathering? (pp. 1403–1404)

Conclusions

Finally, you might consider ending your Discussion section with yet another recap of the study. For example, Tsaousides et al. (2009) finished their discussion with a major subhead Conclusion, which reads in its entirety as follows:

> The present findings highlight the importance of domain-specific and general self-efficacy in perceptions of QoL [quality of life]. Both study hypotheses were supported, as both employment-related and general self-efficacy were associated with perceptions of QoL and need attainment, and both were better predictors than traditionally important contributors such as income and employment. These findings were consistent with Cicerone and Azulay (2007) in terms of the importance of self-efficacy on well-being, and with Levack et al. (2004), Opperman (2004), and Tsaousides et al. (2008) in terms of the importance of subjective self-appraisals of employment in evaluating quality of life post-TBI [traumatic brain injury]. The clinical implications for professionals working in the field of rehabilitation are that increasing confidence in work-related abilities and enhancing self-efficacy among individuals with TBI may facilitate return to work and will certainly have an impact on perceptions of well-being. (pp. 304–305)

This statement hits on almost all of the recommendations included in the JARS, and it serves as a nice complement to the study's abstract for readers who do not wish to delve too deeply into the details.

Discussion of Studies With Experimental Manipulations

If your study involved an experimental manipulation, your discussion should include

- discussion of results, taking into account the mechanism by which the manipulation or intervention was intended to work (causal pathways) or alternative mechanisms, and
- if an intervention was involved, discussion of the success of and barriers to implementing the intervention and the fidelity of implementation.

If your study involved an experimental manipulation, especially if it was an intervention meant to change problem behaviors, there are some other recommendations made in the JARS regarding issues that should be addressed in the Discussion section. First, the JARS suggests you discuss the mechanisms that mediate the relationship between cause and effect. For example, how is it that different labels lead to different ratings of the same fragrance? Does the label trigger positive or negative memories? Does it alter the length of time participants inhale?

Amir et al. (2009) found evidence for the following causal mechanisms in their study of attention training:

> Although accumulating evidence suggests that computerized attention training procedures are efficacious in reducing symptoms of anxiety in treatment-seeking samples, little is known about the attentional mechanisms underlying clinical improvement. . . . The results suggested that the AMP [attention modification program] facilitated participants' ability to disengage their attention from social threat cues from pre- to posttraining. (p. 970)

However, they were careful to point out the limitations of their proposed explanation:

> The results of the mediation analysis, however, should be interpreted with caution, given that change in the putative mediator (attention bias) and change in social anxiety symptoms were assessed at the same time, and temporal precedence was therefore not established. Thus, although causal inferences can be made about change in attention resulting from the AMP, we cannot make such claims about the relation between change in attention and symptom change. (Amir et al., 2009, p. 970)

In addition, they used this limitation to call for future research:

> In future research, investigators should administer assessments of attention at multiple points during the course of treatment to better address these issues. (Amir et al., 2009, p. 970)

For experiments, the discussion of the generalizability (external validity) of the findings should take into account

- the characteristics of the intervention,
- how and what outcomes were measured,
- length of follow-up,
- incentives, and
- compliance rates.

When your study involves the evaluation of an intervention, there can be unique aspects of the study related to the generalizability of the findings that need to be addressed in the Discussion section. For example, Norman et al.'s (2008) smoking intervention proved to be generally successful:

> This study demonstrates that an intervention designed around a website supported by additional motivational components can be integrated into schools to support smoking cessation and prevention in an engaging manner. Through the use of multiple learning channels, the *Smoking Zine* was able to significantly reduce the likelihood that an adolescent would take up smoking over 6 months when compared with similar students in the control condition, especially with regard to adoption of heavy smoking. (p. 807)

However, the way the researchers chose to introduce the intervention might have placed limits on their ability to generalize to other means of implementation:

> School-based trials typically randomize classes; we chose to randomize participants at the individual level because of the personalized nature of the intervention. Doing so introduced the possibility that students would share lessons learned with their peers. . . . Integrating the intervention into regular classroom activities potentially reduced its novelty and the likelihood of extramural discussion. (Norman et al., 2008, p. 807)

Norman et al.'s first concern, often referred to as *treatment diffusion*, would reduce the effect of the intervention because students in the treatment condition shared what they learned with students in the control condition. Their second concern would limit the impact of the treatment. In addition, Norman et al. pointed out a concern about compliance rates:

> Another area worthy of consideration is the fact that fewer smokers completed the 6-month trial compared with nonsmokers. A potential reason could be attributed to complications arising from increased engagement in risk behaviors among the smokers. . . . These risk behaviors may have contributed to an increased absenteeism rate at school, making follow-up more difficult. (pp. 807–808)

Amir et al. (2009) highlighted their use of a 4-month follow-up:

> Assessments completed approximately 4 months after completion of the postassessment revealed that participants maintained symptom reduction after completing the training, suggesting that the beneficial effects of the AMP were enduring (see also Schmidt et al., 2009). However, follow-up data should be interpreted with caution because assessors and participants were no longer blind to participant condition. Future research should investigate the long-term impact of the attention training procedure, including an assessment of symptoms as well as attention bias. (p. 969)

Vadasy and Sanders (2008) provided a discussion of the limitations of their study that almost directly paralleled the recommendations of the JARS. First, the summary:

> The present study evaluated the direct and indirect effects of a supplemental, paraeducator-implemented repeated reading intervention (*Quick Reads*) with incidental word-level instruction for second and third graders with low fluency skill. Results show clearly that students benefited from this intervention in terms of word reading and fluency gains. Specifically, our models that tested for direct treatment effects indicated that tutored students had significantly higher pretest–posttest gains in word reading accuracy and fluency. (Vadasy & Sanders, 2008, pp. 281–286)

Then, they addressed how their findings related to the work of others. Note how this excerpt also addresses some of the JARS recommendations regarding discussions of generalization (e.g., multiple outcomes, characteristics of the intervention including treatment fidelity), but here the authors pointed out the strengths of their study in this regard:

> This study specifically addressed limitations in previous research on repeated reading interventions. First, students were randomly assigned to conditions. (Vadasy & Sanders, 2008, p. 287)

They used multiple outcomes:

> Second, we considered multiple outcomes, including word reading accuracy and efficiency as well as fluency rate and comprehension outcomes. (Vadasy & Sanders, 2008, p. 287)

Their treatment was implemented with high fidelity, using the types of professionals likely to be used in "real life" and in the real-life setting:

> Third, because this was an efficacy trial, the intervention was implemented with a high degree of fidelity by paraeducators who were potential typical end users, and in school settings that reflected routine practice conditions. (Vadasy & Sanders, 2008, p. 287)[2]

Their treatment was well specified:

> Fourth, the 15-week intervention was considerably more intense than the repeated reading interventions described in many previous studies. Fifth, the particular repeated reading intervention, *Quick Reads,* is unusually well specified in terms of text features and reading procedures often hypothesized to influence fluency outcomes. (Vadasy & Sanders, 2008, pp. 287–288)

Finally, they discussed some limitations. First, for theoretical interpretation, the intervention might not have involved reading instruction only:

> Findings from this study should be considered in light of several limitations. First, although the intervention used in this study was primarily characterized as repeated reading, a small portion (up to 5 min) of each of the tutoring sessions included incidental alphabetic instruction and word-level scaffolding. (Vadasy & Sanders, 2008, p. 287)

The characteristics of students may have been unique:

> Second, students entered this study with a wide range of pretest fluency levels that reflected teacher referral patterns; nevertheless, students ranged from the 10th to the 60th percentiles on PRF [passage-reading fluency] performance, similar to students served in repeated reading programs. (Vadasy & Sanders, 2008, p. 287)

Note that Vadasy and Sanders here raised a possible shortcoming of their study that they then provided evidence to refute. This can be an important strategy for you to use: Think of concerns that might occur to your readers, raise them yourself, and provide your take on whether you think they are legitimate and why.

---

[2]An *efficacy trial* is an experiment that is undertaken to demonstrate that a particular intervention can have its intended effect. It is typically followed by an *effectiveness trial* that is meant to show that the intervention effect can be produced under "real-world" conditions.

The classroom observations may have limited the researchers' ability to describe the causal mediating mechanisms:

> Third, we observed classroom instruction only twice during the intervention. As others have demonstrated . . . dimensions of classroom instruction that our coding system did not capture, such as individual student engagement or quality of instruction . . . , may have influenced student outcomes. (Vadasy & Sanders, 2008, p. 287)

Some teachers refused to participate, so some results may apply only to teachers who were open to full participation:

> Fourth, our findings on classroom literacy instruction are based on data excluding six teachers (and their students). It is possible that these teachers' refusal to participate reflects a systematic difference in their literacy instruction; however, outcomes of students within these classrooms did not reliably differ from outcomes of students whose teachers were observed. (Vadasy & Sanders, 2008, p. 287)

Finally, some important variables may have gone unmeasured:

> A final limitation of this study is that many variables expected to contribute to comprehension gains were not accounted for in this study, including vocabulary knowledge, strategy skills, and general language skills. (Vadasy & Sanders, 2008, p. 287)

Perhaps one of the most interesting discussions of limitations was by Vinnars, Thormählen, Gallop, Norén, and Barber (2009). They found that their experimental treatment for people with personality disorder did not outperform the control treatment:

> This study explored the extent to which manualized psychodynamic psychotherapy was superior to ordinary clinical treatment as conducted in the community in Scandinavia in improving maladaptive personality functioning in patients with any *DSM–IV* PD diagnosis. We did not find any significant difference between the two treatments, suggesting perhaps that the format of treatment (i.e., whether it was manualized psychodynamic or ordinary clinical treatment) did not seem to differentially affect change in personality. The one exception was for neuroticism, and this was only during follow-up. (Vinnars et al., 2009, p. 370)

So what do we learn from this study?

> In summary, the results from these studies indicate that improvement in interpersonal problems is possible. However, it is hard to predict in advance what specific treatment, what treatment length, or for what specific sample of patients these interpersonal problems will improve. (Vinnars et al., 2009, p. 372)

> You should describe the clinical or practical significance of outcomes and the basis for these interpretations.

It is especially important when reporting the results of an evaluation of an intervention to delve into the clinical or practical significance of the findings. In the case of Amir et al.'s (2009) evaluation, the practical implications were most evident because of the short duration of the treatment:

> These findings speak to the utility of the AMP, given the brevity of the intervention (eight sessions over 4 weeks, 20 min each) and absence of therapist contact. Although empirically supported treatments for SP [social phobia] already exist, many people do not have access to therapists trained in CBT, whereas others opt not to take medication for their symptoms. . . . The ease of delivery of the current intervention suggests that the AMP may serve as a transportable and widely accessible treatment for individuals with SP who are unable to or choose not to access existing treatments. (p. 970)

Vadasy and Sanders (2008) drew some clear practice implications for reading instruction:

> Findings support clear benefits from the opportunities students had to engage in oral reading practice during the classroom reading block. When students read aloud, teachers have opportunities to detect student difficulties, including poor prosody, decoding errors, and limited comprehension reflected in dysfluent reading. Teachers can use this information to adjust instruction for individual students and provide effective corrections and scaffolding. (p. 287)

Ordering Material in the Discussion

One of the more difficult chores I had in writing this book was taking apart the Discussion sections of the example reports so that I could illustrate the items in the JARS. Other than the placement of the restatement of goals and summary of findings, what elements of a Discussion section should go where is a matter of the individual authors' preferences and the unique demands of the topic and findings. Therefore, do not get hung up on preparing your discussion in the same sequence I have here. Just be sure to include discussion of the elements called for in the JARS. Where in the Discussion section you cover each and in what depth should be dictated by what order will help your readers make sense of your findings and make your message clear. Clarity and completeness rule the day.

6

Reporting a Meta-Analysis

The same concerns that have led to more detailed reporting standards for new data collections have led to similar efforts to establish standards for the reporting of other types of research. In particular, attention has been focused on the reporting of meta-analyses, and the American Psychological Association group that developed the Journal Article Reporting Standards (JARS) also developed the Meta-Analysis Reporting Standards (MARS; see Table A6.1).

In this chapter, I do not try to explain each of the items in the MARS. That would take another book, and many books already exist for learning how to conduct a research synthesis and meta-analysis (e.g., Borenstein, Hedges, Higgins, & Rothstein, 2009; Cooper, 2010; Cooper, Hedges, & Valentine, 2009). Instead, I focus on the most important items in the MARS.[1]

Critical Elements to Report About a Meta-Analysis

Introduction

The introduction to your meta-analysis should include a clear statement of the question or relation(s) under investigation, including

- types of predictor and outcome measures used and their psychometric characteristics and
- populations to which the question or relation is relevant.

---

[1]How did I know which items to pick? In the course of preparing a book chapter, Amy Dent and I (Cooper & Dent, 2011) conducted a survey of the 74 members of the Society for Research Synthesis Methodology. The society's members were asked to rate the importance of each MARS item on a scale from 1 (*generally, it is unnecessary in my field for researchers to report this information*) to 10 (*generally, it would be considered unethical in my field not to include this information in the report*). Of the society's members, 42 (57%) responded to the survey. I discuss those items that received a score of 10 from 50% or more of the society's members.

It is important to address three MARS items in your introduction. These items call for a clear statement of the research problem, a description of the predictor (independent) and outcome (dependent) variables of primary interest, and a description of the populations to which the question is relevant. These items are no different from those most important to include in the introduction to a report based on new data. The MARS items simply reiterate how critical a clear problem statement is to any scientific endeavor.

As a running example for this chapter, I refer to a research synthesis by Grabe, Ward, and Hyde (2008). These authors reported the results of a meta-analysis on the role of mass media in the body image concerns of women. They stated their research question plainly and simply:

> Why is it that so many girls and young women are dissatisfied with their bodies, regardless of their size? (Grabe et al., 2008, p. 460)

This statement also makes clear what population was relevant to the question. Media, their conceptual independent variable, was "movies, magazines, and television programs" (Grabe et al., 2008, p. 460). The conceptual definition for their outcome variable was not as simple:

> What is perhaps the greatest challenge to drawing sound conclusions from this large and growing literature is that results may vary depending on the particular dimension of body image or related eating behavior that is being measured. (Grabe et al., 2008, p. 462)

Grabe et al.'s (2008) problem highlights an important difference between meta-analysis and primary research and why these conceptual definitions are so critical. Researchers collecting new data typically gather or manipulate only one or two operational definitions of the same construct. For example, they may expose women to images of thin people in a film and then ask them how satisfied they are with their own bodies: one manipulation of the conceptual variable—media—and one measure of body-image concerns. Meta-analysts, however, may come across numerous operational definitions of the variables of interest. In addition to satisfaction measures, Grabe et al. discovered measures of body image based on preoccupation with the body, internalization of thin ideals, and behaviors related to eating. They had to provide a multidimensional scheme for measures of body image and then examine the effects of media on four different clusters of body-image concerns. Their intention to do this and the rationale for it were clearly laid out in their introduction.

Inclusion Criteria

Your report of the inclusion criteria should include

- operational characteristics of independent (predictor) and dependent (outcome) variable(s),
- eligible participant populations,
- eligible research design features (e.g., random assignment only, minimal sample size), and
- time period in which studies needed to be conducted.

The three items on the MARS most critical to criteria for including and excluding studies are (a) the operational definitions of independent (predictor) and dependent (outcome) variables, (b) a description of the eligible participant populations, and (c) the features of eligible research designs.[2] It is not surprising that the most important inclusion and exclusion criteria correspond to the conceptual issues laid out in the introduction.

For measures of body image, Grabe et al. (2008) mentioned 14 standardized measures (plus a catchall category) used to assess women's dissatisfaction with their bodies. After each measure, they provided a reference so that readers could find more information about it:

> In the category of body dissatisfaction we focused on measures that assess the evaluative component of body image, that is, satisfaction or dissatisfaction with the body. The following scales were classified as measures that assessed dissatisfaction with the body and were included in the current review: (a) the Visual Analogue Scales (Heinberg & Thompson, 1995) . . . and (n) the Body Esteem Scale (Mendelson & White, 1985). In addition to these scales, a variety of scales that were not standardized but were specifically described as measuring global body dissatisfaction were included. (Grabe et al., 2008, p. 463)

Providing these references is good practice and permits you to spend less space describing each measure, instrument, or procedure included in the meta-analysis. Grabe et al. (2008) used the same approach to report the measures of preoccupation with the body, internalization of body image ideals, and eating behaviors. For media use, they included correlational studies that asked women about media use or media exposure but left out studies that simply asked participants how influenced they were by the media.

When conducting a meta-analysis (or any research synthesis, for that matter), you will find much more variety in the data collection procedures than in any report of a single new study. This is why spelling out the inclusion criteria is so important. Grabe et al. (2008) included all of the body image measures they found. For media exposure, however, they drew the line at indirect measures:

> Because our goal was to test directly the association between the use of media and women's body image and related concerns, we included only those studies that investigated media use or media exposure, as opposed to self-report of media influence (i.e., perceived pressure from media to change exercise or eating patterns). (Grabe et al., 2008, p. 463)

The important thing, from the point of view of the MARS, is that the authors told readers why studies were included in the analysis. With this information, readers can agree or disagree with their decision.

Meta-analysts also must tell readers the characteristics of participants who were and were not considered relevant to the research question. Grabe et al. (2008) did not explicitly define "girls and young women" (p. 460), but their table containing the characteristics of studies included in the meta-analysis has a column that provides the median age

---

[2]These were followed closely in the survey by the need to include any time period restrictions. For example, Grabe et al. (2008) reported that they included studies published between 1975 and January 2007.

of the samples. Also, because issues with body image are culture bound, they explained that they included only studies conducted in four English-speaking countries.

> Search limits restricted the results to articles published in English between 1975 and January 2007 and included studies conducted in English-speaking countries (e.g., the United States, Canada, Great Britain, and Australia). Appearance ideals can vary widely across cultures, yet little research has been conducted in other cultures. We therefore restricted ourselves to these four closely related cultures in which there is substantial research and often shared media. (Grabe et al., 2008, p. 464)

Without this information, readers could not assess to whom the results apply, nor could they argue that participants who were included or excluded should not have been.

Grabe et al. (2008) first addressed the issue of eligible research designs in the introduction to their meta-analysis. They devoted nearly a whole page to telling readers that two designs had been used in media and body-image studies. Experimental studies manipulated whether girls and young women were exposed to thin media models (or other images) and then tested to see whether participants exposed to thin images felt worse about their bodies. Correlational studies used naturalistic data to test the relationship between exposure to media and body image. Grabe et al. then used research design as a moderator variable in their meta-analysis. As in new data collections, a clear description of methods allows the reader to gauge the fit among the research designs, how the design was implemented, and the inferences drawn by the meta-analysts.

Literature Search

> Your description of the literature search should include
>
> - treatment of unpublished studies and
> - reference and citation databases searched.

Reference and citation databases searched. Your first step in finding studies relevant to the topic of your meta-analysis likely will be to search computerized reference databases and citation indexes. The MARS calls for a full accounting of which databases you consulted and the keywords you used to enter them. This matters because different reference databases cover different journals and other sources of documents. Also, some reference databases contain only published research, whereas others contain both published and unpublished studies, and others include only unpublished research. It will be difficult for readers to consider what studies you might have missed if they do not know which databases you used. Equally important, without this information, it would be difficult for others to reproduce the results of your meta-analysis.

Grabe et al. (2008) described their search of reference databases as follows:

> A computerized database search of PsycINFO and the Web of Science was conducted to generate a pool of potential articles. To identify all articles that investigated the link between media use and body image concerns, the words *body image, media, television, advertising,* and *magazines* were used as key terms in

the literature search. These broad terms were selected to capture the wide range of research that has been conducted. Search limits restricted the results to articles published in English between 1975 and January 2007. (p. 464)

A host of other literature retrieval strategies are available (see Cooper, 2010). Some will be more relevant to your search than others. The MARS recommends that you list them all. Note as well that Grabe et al. (2008) explicitly stated the key terms they entered into the databases and two other restrictions on their search.

Treatment of unpublished studies. Your decision to include or exclude unpublished research in your literature search is of critical importance because unpublished studies typically reveal smaller effect sizes than do published ones, on average by about one third (Lipsey & Wilson, 1993). So, including only published studies can make relationships appear stronger than they would if all of the studies were included. That is why Grabe et al. (2008) reported that they included dissertations that they obtained via interlibrary loan (p. 464).

Meta-analysts who exclude unpublished research often say they do so because these studies have not undergone the peer review process and therefore may be of lesser quality. However, there is good evidence that publication is often not the final stop for much research, regardless of its quality (cf. Cooper, DeNeve, & Charlton, 1997). For example, if you completed the hypothetical study of labeling effects on perfume as a master's thesis or doctoral dissertation and you then went to work for a perfume company, you might never submit it for publication. Likewise, a report for a government agency might appear in a reference database but never be submitted for publication (even if it underwent peer review before the agency released it). Also, studies are often turned down by journals for reasons other than quality. Journals sometimes use the novelty of the contribution as a criterion for publication, and this is of no concern to meta-analysts. Finally, a report submitted for publication may be turned down because the statistical test fails to reject the null hypothesis. Sometimes authors interested in publication do not even submit reports for publication when the null hypothesis is not rejected. To meta-analysts, the statistical significance of the individual finding is irrelevant; they want all of the evidence.

Again, from the MARS perspective, whether you include unpublished literature in your meta-analysis is not the issue of import. What is critical is that you provide a clear description and justification for your decision.

Measure of Effect

Your description of the effect sizes in your meta-analysis should report

- effect-size calculating formulas (e.g., means and standard deviations, use of univariate F to r transform),
- corrections made to effect sizes (e.g., small sample bias, correction for unequal sample sizes),
- effect-size averaging and/or weighting method(s), and
- how studies with more than one effect size were handled.

Effect-size metric(s). In Chapter 4, I discussed what an effect-size estimate is and the different effect-size metrics. In a meta-analysis, it is especially critical that you tell readers what formulas you used to calculate effect sizes and whether you applied any corrections. Someday, every primary researcher will report effect sizes, and this will become less of an issue. Today, meta-analysts often have to calculate the effect sizes themselves. They use a host of formulas; the most prominent of these require access to means and standard deviations so meta-analysts can calculate d indexes. In many instances, however, they must estimate effect sizes from inference test values (e.g., t tests or F tests) and sample sizes or degrees of freedom (for many approaches to estimating effect sizes, see Borenstein, 2009; Fleiss & Berlin, 2009). Sometimes, meta-analysts can plug these numbers into software programs that do the calculations for them. If you had to estimate effect sizes in your meta-analysis, it is important to describe the formulas or the name of the program that you used. Grabe et al. (2008) described their effect-size calculations as follows:

> Formulas for the effect size d were taken from Hedges and Becker (1986). When means and standard deviations were available, the effect size was computed as the mean body image score for the control condition minus the mean body image score for the experimental condition, divided by the pooled within-groups standard deviation. Therefore, negative effect sizes represent a more negative outcome (e.g., more body dissatisfaction) for women exposed to thin-ideal media than for women in the control condition. Means and standard deviations were available for 74 (93%) of the experimental studies. When means and standard deviations for experimental studies were not available, the effect size was calculated from reported t or F tests. (p. 468)

Corrections to effect sizes. Sometimes, effect sizes are adjusted to remove some form of bias in estimation. Most frequently, this is small sample bias, but you can also remove biases due to artifacts, such as the reliability of the measure or a restriction on the range of scores in the sample. Grabe et al. (2008) wrote,

> Because effect sizes tend to be upwardly biased when based on small sample sizes, effect sizes were corrected for bias in the estimation of population effect sizes using the formula provided by Hedges (1981). (p. 468)

Effect-size averaging and weighting method(s). Once each effect size has been calculated, meta-analysts next average the effects that estimate the same relationship. Grabe et al. (2008) averaged 20 effect sizes relating media exposure to eating disorder symptoms. It is generally accepted that the individual effect sizes should be weighted by the inverse of the variance (on the basis of the number of participants in their respective samples) before they are averaged. Sometimes, however, unweighted effect sizes are presented. Weighted and unweighted effect sizes can differ in magnitude, sometimes by a lot.[3] For

---

[3]The difference between a weighted and an unweighted average effect size depends on the strength of the relationship between the effect size and the sample size. If larger effects are associated with smaller sample sizes (a not uncommon occurrence in meta-analysis because of bias against the null hypothesis), the unweighted average effect size would be larger than the weighted average.

this reason, the MARS recommends that the procedures you used to average effect sizes be included in your meta-analysis report. Grabe et al. (2008) reported,

> All effect-size analyses were weighted analyses (i.e., each effect size was weighted by an inverted variance. (p. 468)

How studies with more than one effect size were handled. A frequent problem for meta-analysts occurs when researchers give multiple measures of the same construct to the same sample of participants and then report multiple effect-size estimates. For example, suppose you found a correlational study with three measures of media exposure (movies, television, and magazines) and three measures of body satisfaction. You might find in the report nine effect sizes, even though the effects all relate to the same underlying constructs and were collected from the same people. These effect sizes are not statistically independent and therefore cannot be treated as such when you combine the effect sizes across all studies (some of them might have reported only one effect size and therefore would get only one ninth of the weight). Unless you take this into account, studies with more measures would influence the average effect size more, and the assumption that effect-size estimates are independent will be violated when you calculate a confidence interval for the average effect size.

Meta-analysts use several approaches to handle dependent effect sizes. Some meta-analysts use the study as the unit of analysis by taking the mean or median effect size to represent the study. Others use a shifting unit of analysis (Cooper, 2010).[4] Finally, there are more sophisticated (but less frequently used) statistical approaches to solving the problem of dependent effect-size estimates (Gleser & Olkin, 2009).

Which techniques you use can have a large impact on (a) the estimated average magnitude of the effect size, (b) the estimated variance in effect sizes, and (c) the power of tests to uncover moderators of effects. For this reason, the MARS recommends that meta-analysts clearly and completely report how nonindependent estimates of effect were handled.

Variation Among Effect Sizes

The assumptions meta-analysts make about the sources of variance in effect sizes require them to grapple with some fairly complex issues. In a nutshell, you have three choices: a fixed-effects model, a random-effects model, or a mixed-effects model. A fixed-effects model assumes that each effect size's variance reflects sampling error of participants only, that is, error solely due to participant differences. In a random-effects model, other features of studies, such as their location, measures, experimenters, and so on, are assumed to be sampled as well, creating additional random influences. Hedges and Vevea (1998) stated that a fixed-effect model should be used when your goal is "to make inferences only about the effect-size parameters in the set of studies

---

[4]Here, each effect size associated with a study is coded as if it were independent. These are averaged prior to entry into the analysis when estimating the overall effect size. This way, each study contributes one value. However, in analyses that examine moderators, each study could contribute one effect size to the estimate of each moderator grouping's average effect size. Therefore, in the media and eating disorder example, all nine correlations would be averaged before entry into the estimation of the overall relationship strength. Three correlations would be averaged (across measures of eating disorder symptoms) within the three types of media when the influence of media type on the relationship is examined and reaveraged across media types when eating disorder symptoms are examined.

that are observed (or a set of studies identical to the observed studies except for uncertainty associated with the sampling of subjects)" (p. 3). You should use the random-effects model when you want to make inferences about a broader population of people and studies.

The results produced by random-effects models are typically more conservative than those of fixed-effects models. Random-effects models typically estimate more variability around average effect sizes and, therefore, are less likely to reveal statistically significant effects. Finally, the two models also can generate different average effect sizes, again depending on the relationship between the size of effects and the size of samples. In a mixed-effects model, some variance is assumed to be systematic (that associated with the moderator variable) and some is assumed to be random (that due to truly chance factors).

For these reasons, the MARS states that it is essential that you report whether you used a fixed-effects, random-effects, or mixed-effects model when you (a) averaged your effect sizes, (b) calculated their variance, and (c) conducted moderator analyses. Without knowing this information, it is impossible for readers (and you) to interpret your results. For example, Grabe et al. (2008) wrote the following:

> We used mixed-effects models, which assume that effect-size variance can be explained by both systematic and random components. . . . Mixed-effects models assume that the effects of between-study variables are systematic but that there is a remaining unmeasured random effect in the effect-size distribution in addition to sampling error. As is done in random-effects models, a random-effects variance component (derived from the residual homogeneity value after the moderators are taken into account) is estimated and added to the standard error associated with each effect size, and inverted variance weights are calculated. (pp. 468–469)

Although this description is very technical and requires considerable knowledge of meta-analysis to decode, it provides a complete description of what was done and why.

Tables

The tables in your meta-analysis should include

- overall characteristics of the database (e.g., number of studies with different research designs);
- overall effect-size estimates, including measures of uncertainty (e.g., confidence and/or credibility intervals) and results of moderator and mediator analyses (analyses of subsets of studies), including
  - number of studies and total sample sizes for each moderator analysis and
  - assessment of interrelations among variables used for moderator and mediator analyses; and
- description of information for each included study, including effect size and sample size.

It is not surprising that a table that summarizes the results of the meta-analysis is de rigueur. In most cases, a table with information on your tests of a moderator variable is also needed. This table would include, at least, the number of studies in each moderator category and effect sizes and confidence intervals for each category. A table listing the results for the individual studies going into the analyses may also be called for. However, space limitations may dictate that these tables not be included in the published version of the article.

Grabe et al. (2008) presented a table listing characteristics of each study. It spanned three and a half double-columned pages. I do not reproduce that here. Suffice it to say that the columns of the table presented the following:

- first author and year of appearance of the study,
- effect size,
- sample size (experimental and control group separately or total sample for correlational studies),
- mean age of the sample,
- study design,
- media type,
- type of control, and
- measurement instrument.

Table 6.1 presents Grabe et al.'s table for overall findings, and Table 6.2 presents one of their tables reporting moderator analyses. Details of how to construct these tables in your manuscript can be found in the *Publication Manual* (American Psychological Association, 2010b, sections 5.07–5.19, pp. 128–150).

Table 6.1. Example of Overall Effect Sizes

Summary of Mean Effect Sizes for Mixed-Effects Analysis

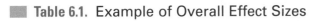

Measure type	No. studies	d	95% CI	Q_T
Body image dissatisfaction	90	−.28	[−.21, −.35]	100.34
Internalization	23	−.39	[−.33, −.44]	66.15*
Eating behaviors and beliefs	20	−.30	[−.24, −.36]	46.30***

Note. A negative *d* indicates that the control group scored higher than the experimental group on negative body image. CI = confidence interval; Q_T = total heterogeneity. From "The Role of the Media in Body Image Concerns Among Women: A Meta-Analysis of Experimental and Correlational Studies," by S. Grabe, L. M. Ward, & J. S. Hyde, 2008, *Psychological Bulletin, 134*, p. 469. Copyright 2008 by the American Psychological Association.
*p < .05. ***p < .001.

■ **Table 6.2.** Example of Moderators of Effect Sizes

Variables Potentially Moderating the Link Between Media Exposure and Eating Behaviors and Beliefs

Variable	Between-groups Q	No. studies	d	Within-group Q
Study design	0.84			
Experimental		8	−.36	21.91**
Correlational		12	−.28	28.46**
Age group in years	6.43*			
Adolescent (ages 10–18)		4	−.20	4.38
Young adult/adult (ages 19–32)		16	−.35	40.40***
Media type	4.0*			
Television		7	−.29	22.42**
Magazines		11	−.26	24.70**
Generalized media		2	−.50	0.09
Publication status	11.42***			
Published		17	−.27	37.72**
Not published		3	−.99	2.07
Publication year	0.09			
1990–1999		8	−.30	25.81***
2000–2005		12	−.28	25.31**

Note. Q = heterogeneity. From "The Role of the Media in Body Image Concerns Among Women: A Meta-Analysis of Experimental and Correlational Studies," by S. Grabe, L. M. Ward, & J. S. Hyde, 2008, *Psychological Bulletin, 134*, p. 470. Copyright 2008 by the American Psychological Association.
*$p < .05$. **$p < .01$. ***$p < .001$.

Discussion

Your interpretation of the results (i.e., discussion) of your meta-analysis should cover

- a statement of major findings;
- consideration of alternative explanations for observed results;
- the generalizability of conclusions (e.g., relevant populations, treatment variations, dependent (outcome) variables, research designs, etc.);
- the general limitations (including assessment of the quality of studies included);
- implications and interpretation for theory, policy, or practice; and
- guidelines for future research.

Similar to the elements of the introduction, the items on the MARS stating what is needed in the Discussion section look much like the items recommended for reports of new primary research. Grabe et al. (2008) began their discussion by stating,

> This meta-analysis represents a systematic inquiry into the overall associations of thin-ideal media exposure and three main areas of women's body image and related concerns. The results show consistent associations across both experimental and correlational designs and across multiple measures of women's body image and eating behaviors and beliefs. Thus, these findings provide strong support for the notion that exposure to mass media depicting the thin-ideal body is related to women's vulnerability to disturbances related to body image. (p. 470)

Concerning alternative explanations, Grabe et al. (2008) appealed to the fact that the finding was consistent across both experimental and correlational evidence. This suggests that alternative explanations are not many:

> The finding from the experimental literature in the current review (57% of studies) provides evidence of a link between exposure to thin-ideal media images and body dissatisfaction in women. The similar outcome found in the correlational literature supports this finding and suggests that this phenomenon also operates outside a laboratory context. Prospective studies will be important in fully assessing the role of the media in women's vulnerability to disturbances related to body image. (Grabe et al., 2008, p. 470)

This final sentence indicates Grabe et al. thought future studies would be most valuable if they included longitudinal measures, a design feature rarely used in past research. Implicitly, they were acknowledging that experimental studies were of short duration and that this might influence the impact of media images on women. How should we interpret the findings?

> The current findings can be interpreted in the context of other, more well established areas of media research. For example, researchers have focused extensively on the influence of violent media on the aggressive behavior of youth. . . . experimental studies demonstrated that brief exposure to violent video games led to an immediate increase in aggressive behavior, whereas the correlational studies linked repeated exposure to violent video games to a variety of types of real-world aggressive behavior. . . . Thin-ideal media research is much newer and inferences must therefore be more modest, but the media violence research provides a roadmap for ways in which research can proceed. (Grabe et al., 2008, p. 471)

What does it all mean?

> The findings from this study can inform prevention and intervention efforts particularly in the areas of education and advertising. With respect to education, media literacy can be used to teach girls and women to become more active, critical consumers of appearance-related media. . . . Perhaps of greater benefit

> would be to reduce the emphasis on an unrealistically thin ideal that is perpetuated through the objectification of women's bodies in the media. (Grabe et al., 2008, pp. 471–472)

However, Grabe et al. were careful not to claim too much:

> Despite the contributions of the present study, there are limitations that future research may want to address. First, much of what is known about women's body dissatisfaction is based largely on White samples. . . . Second, although we believe that the correlational data enhanced the validity of the experimental findings by providing data on actual media diets, the nature of correlational data does not permit identification of the prospective contributions of media to the development of negative body image. . . . Third, research on the potential consequences of thin-ideal media needs to be extended to include other outcomes, such as obesity and body self-consciousness. . . . Finally, it is interesting to note that in a small percentage of studies there was a positive effect of media on women's body image concerns, suggesting that some women actually feel better about themselves after viewing media images. . . . It is possible that women who are consciously addressing their body image (e.g., restricting calories) or are already satisfied with their bodies feel elevated satisfaction in the presence of the appearance-related cues provided by the media. However, given that the number of studies in this area were few, interpretations of this finding are tentative. (Grabe et al., 2008, p. 472)

Finally, what are the policy implications?

> New policies adopted in Spain and Italy, and more tentatively by the Council of Fashion Designers of America, that exclude hyperthin women from modeling may be helpful not only to the models themselves but also to millions of girls and women who view these images. (Grabe et al., 2008, p. 472)

In sum then, the MARS recommends that the introduction and Discussion sections of a meta-analysis contain information not unlike their counterparts in reports of primary research. Where the two forms of research differ is "up the middle," in their descriptions of methods and results, where the methodologies are unique.

Appendix 6.1:
Meta-Analysis Reporting Standards (MARS)

Table A6.1. Meta-Analysis Reporting Standards (MARS): Information Recommended for Inclusion in Manuscripts Reporting Meta-Analyses

Paper section and topic	Description
Title	Make it clear that the report describes a research synthesis and include "meta-analysis," if applicable
	Footnote funding source(s)
Abstract	The problem or relation(s) under investigation
	Study eligibility criteria
	Type(s) of participants included in primary studies
	Meta-analysis methods (indicating whether a fixed or random model was used)
	Main results (including the more important effect sizes and any important moderators of these effect sizes)
	Conclusions (including limitations)
	Implications for theory, policy, and/or practice
Introduction	Clear statement of the question or relation(s) under investigation:
	Historical background
	Theoretical, policy, and/or practical issues related to the question or relation(s) of interest
	Rationale for the selection and coding of potential moderators and mediators of results
	Types of study designs used in the primary research, their strengths and weaknesses
	Types of predictor and outcome measures used, their psychometric characteristics
	Populations to which the question or relation is relevant
	Hypotheses, if any
Method	
Inclusion and exclusion criteria	Operational characteristics of independent (predictor) and dependent (outcome) variable(s)
	Eligible participant populations
	Eligible research design features (e.g., random assignment only, minimal sample size)
	Time period in which studies needed to be conducted
	Geographical and/or cultural restrictions
Moderator and mediator analyses	Definition of all coding categories used to test moderators or mediators of the relation(s) of interest
Search strategies	Reference and citation databases searched
	Registries (including prospective registries) searched:
	Keywords used to enter databases and registries
	Search software used and version
	Time period in which studies needed to be conducted, if applicable
	Other efforts to retrieve all available studies:
	Listservs queried
	Contacts made with authors (and how authors were chosen)
	Reference lists of reports examined
	Method of addressing reports in languages other than English
	Process for determining study eligibility:
	Aspects of reports were examined (i.e., title, abstract, and/or full text)
	Number and qualifications of relevance judges
	Indication of agreement
	How disagreements were resolved
	Treatment of unpublished studies

■ **Table A6.1.** *(Continued)*

Paper section and topic	Description

Coding procedures	Number and qualifications of coders (e.g., level of expertise in the area, training)
	Intercoder reliability or agreement
	Whether each report was coded by more than one coder and if so, how disagreements were resolved
	Assessment of study quality:
	    If a quality scale was employed, a description of criteria and the procedures for application
	    If study design features were coded, what these were
	How missing data were handled

Statistical methods	Effect size metric(s):
	    Effect sizes calculating formulas (e.g., Ms and SDs, use of univariate F to r transform)
	    Corrections made to effect sizes (e.g., small sample bias, correction for unequal ns)
	Effect size averaging and/or weighting method(s)
	How effect-size confidence intervals (or standard errors) were calculated
	How effect-size credibility intervals were calculated, if used
	How studies with more than one effect size were handled
	Whether fixed- and/or random-effects models were used and the model choice justification
	How heterogeneity in effect sizes was assessed or estimated
	Ms and SDs for measurement artifacts, if construct-level relationships were the focus
	Tests and any adjustments for data censoring (e.g., publication bias, selective reporting)
	Tests for statistical outliers
	Statistical power of the meta-analysis
	Statistical programs or software packages used to conduct statistical analyses

Results	Number of citations examined for relevance
	List of citations included in the synthesis
	Number of citations relevant on many but not all inclusion criteria excluded from the meta-analysis
	Number of exclusions for each exclusion criterion (e.g., effect size could not be calculated), with examples
	Table giving descriptive information for each included study, including effect size and sample size
	Assessment of study quality, if any
	Tables and/or graphic summaries:
	    Overall characteristics of the database (e.g., number of studies with different research designs)
	    Overall effect-size estimates, including measures of uncertainty (e.g., confidence and/or credibility intervals)
	Results of moderator and mediator analyses (analyses of subsets of studies):
	    Number of studies and total sample sizes for each moderator analysis
	    Assessment of interrelations among variables used for moderator and mediator analyses
	Assessment of bias including possible data censoring

Discussion	Statement of major findings
	Consideration of alternative explanations for observed results:
	    Impact of data censoring
	Generalizability of conclusions:
	    Relevant populations
	    Treatment variations
	    Dependent (outcome) variables
	    Research designs
	General limitations (including assessment of the quality of studies included)
	Implications and interpretation for theory, policy, or practice
	Guidelines for future research

Note. Adapted from "Reporting Standards for Research in Psychology: Why Do We Need Them? What Might They Be?" by APA Publications and Communications Board Working Group on Journal Article Reporting Standards, 2008, *American Psychologist, 63,* pp. 848–849. Copyright 2008 by the American Psychological Association.

7

How the Journal Article Reporting Standards (JARS) and the Meta-Analysis Reporting Standards (MARS) Came to Be and Can Be Used in the Future

In the preceding chapters, I have discussed why researchers need the JARS, how to use the JARS tables in Chapter 1, and how to address the tension between complete reporting and space limitation. In each chapter, I have defined and discussed each item and have presented a rationale for its inclusion. Throughout the chapters, I have provided examples of both good and not-so-good ways to present information recommended in the JARS and in the MARS standards for reporting meta-analyses. In this final chapter, I describe in more detail how the JARS and the MARS came to be and consider how the JARS can be used in the future.[1]

Those of us in the JARS Working Group found that in the past decade, developments in the social, behavioral, and medical sciences had motivated researchers to provide more details when they reported their investigations. In the arenas of public and health policy and practice, we found a growing call for use of *evidence-based decision making*. This call placed a new importance on understanding how research was conducted and what it found. Policymakers and practitioners who were making decisions based at least partly on social science evidence wanted to know how reliable the information was and in what context the data had been collected. In 2006, the American Psychological Association (APA) Presidential Task Force on Evidence-Based Practice (2006) said that "evidence-based practice requires that psychologists recognize the strengths and limitations of evidence obtained from different types of research" (p. 275).

In medicine, members of the JARS Group found the movement toward evidence-based practice was pervasive (see Sackett, Rosenberg, Gray, Haynes, & Richardson,

---

[1]Much of what follows, including some sentences and phrases, is taken from the JARS Group report (APA Publications and Communications Board Working Group on Journal Article Reporting Standards, 2008). This material is used with the permission of the APA Publications and Communications Board and the JARS Group members.

1996). Two events impressed us most. First was the establishment of the Cochrane Collaboration in 1993 (http://www.cochrane.org), an international consortium of medical researchers. This organization has adopted guidelines for conducting and reporting research synthesis and has produced thousands of reviews examining the cumulative evidence on everything from public health initiatives to surgical procedures. Their documents reveal much discussion of reporting standards. On the primary research side was the adoption by the International Committee of Medical Journal Editors (2007) of a policy requiring registration of all medical trials in a public trials registry as a condition of consideration for publication. This indicated a new level of reporting accountability in medical research.

In education, the No Child Left Behind Act of 2001 (2002) required the policies and practices adopted by schools and school districts to be based on scientific evidence. In public policy, a consortium similar to the Cochrane Collaboration had been formed. The Campbell Collaboration (http://www.campbellcollaboration.org) is dedicated to promoting high-quality research syntheses and, along with other organizations (e.g., the Coalition for Evidence-Based Policy; http://www.coalition4evidence.org), was meant to promote government policymaking based on rigorous evidence of program effectiveness. The developers of previous reporting standards (discussed later in this chapter) were often the same individuals who were instrumental in forming these organizations. Collectively, they argued that new transparency in reporting was needed so that accurate judgments could be made about the appropriate inferences and applications derivable from research findings.

The basic research domain within the social and behavioral science disciplines was not without its own calls to action. This was a development close to my own area of interest. As evidence about specific hypotheses and theories accumulates, greater reliance is placed on syntheses of research, especially meta-analyses (Cooper, Hedges, & Valentine, 2009). These research syntheses attempt to summarize cumulative knowledge. New synthesis techniques, in particular meta-analysis, allow researchers to integrate different findings relating to a specific question. However, through either planned or naturally occurring circumstances, varying research designs and/or contexts were used in all studies. Meta-analysts use this variation to find clues to the mediation of basic psychological, behavioral, and social processes uncovered in the individual studies. In meta-analysis, these clues emerge when studies are grouped on the basis of distinctions in their methods and settings and then their results are compared. This synthesis-based evidence is then used to guide the next generation of problems and hypotheses studied in new data collections. Meta-analysts need detailed descriptions of what the primary researchers did. The JARS Group agreed that without complete reporting of methods and results, the utility of studies for purposes of research synthesis and meta-analysis is diminished.

Those of us in the JARS Group viewed these spurs to action as positive developments for the psychological sciences. We wrote,

> The first [use of evidence] provides an unprecedented opportunity for psychological research to play an important role in public and health policy. The second [meta-analysis of basic research] promises a sounder evidence base for explanations of psychological phenomena and a next generation of research that is more focused on resolving critical issues. (APA Publications and Communications Board Working Group on Journal Article Reporting Standards, 2008, p. 840)

The State of the Art Before JARS

The development of JARS began in 2007 with the collection of reporting standards that had been developed by other social science and health organizations. Three efforts quickly came to the attention of the JARS Group. The first is called the Consolidated Standards of Reporting Trials (CONSORT; 2007; http://www.consort-statement.org). CONSORT was developed by an ad hoc group primarily composed of biostatisticians and medical researchers. The CONSORT standards are specific to the reporting of studies that carried out random assignment of participants to conditions. These standards also use language that is most familiar to medical researchers. CONSORT comprises a checklist of study characteristics that should be included in research reports and a flowchart that provides readers with a description of the number of participants as they progress through the study—and by implication the number who drop out—from the time they are deemed eligible for inclusion until the end of the investigation. The use of CONSORT is now required by top medical journals and many other biomedical journals. The JARS Group found that some APA journals had adopted the CONSORT guidelines as well.

The second effort, developed through an initiative of the Centers for Disease Control and Prevention (CDC), is called Transparent Reporting of Evaluations With Nonrandomized Designs (TREND; CDC, 2009). The CDC brought together a group of editors of journals related to public health, including several journals in psychology. TREND contains a 22-item checklist, similar to the checklist in CONSORT but with a specific focus on reporting studies that use quasi-experimental designs, that is, group comparisons in which the groups were established using procedures other than random assignment to place participants in conditions.

In the social sciences, the American Educational Research Association (AERA, 2006) published "Standards for Reporting on Empirical Social Science Research in AERA Publications." These standards encompass a broad range of research designs, including both quantitative and qualitative approaches. AERA divides the standards into eight general areas, including problem formulation; design and logic of the study; sources of evidence; measurement and classification; analysis and interpretation; generalization; ethics in reporting; and title, abstract, and headings. It contains about two dozen general prescriptions for the reporting of studies as well as separate prescriptions for quantitative and qualitative studies.

The JARS Group also examined previous editions of the *Publication Manual of the American Psychological Association*. We discovered that for the past half century, the *Publication Manual* has played an important role in the establishment of reporting standards. The first edition was published in 1952 as a supplement to *Psychological Bulletin* (APA, Council of Editors, 1952). It contained 61 pages printed on 9-in. × 6-in. paper (and cost $1—ah, the good old days!). The principal divisions of manuscripts were Problem, Method, Results, Discussion, and Summary.

Here is what the first *Publication Manual* suggested should be included in each section: The Problem section was to include

- the questions asked and the reasons for asking them and
- when experiments were theory driven, the theoretical propositions that generated the hypotheses, along with the logic of their derivation.

The Method section was to include

- "enough detail to permit the reader to repeat the experiment unless portions of it have been described in other reports which can be cited" (APA, Council of Editors, 1952, p. 9),
- the design and logic of relating the empirical data to theoretical propositions,
- the subjects,
- sampling and control devices,
- the techniques of measurement, and
- any apparatus used.

The Results section was to include

- enough data to justify the conclusions, with special attention to tests of statistical significance and the logic of inference and generalization.

The Discussion section was to include

- limitations of the conclusions,
- the relation of conclusions to other findings and widely accepted points of view, and
- implications for theory or practice.

Also, authors were encouraged to use good grammar and to avoid jargon: "Some writing in psychology gives the impression that long words and obscure expressions are regarded as evidence of scientific status" (APA, Council of Editors, 1952, pp. 11–12; maybe the good old days weren't so good after all!).

These descriptions suggest that little has changed over the past half century in the basic structure and function of a psychology journal article. Of interest, we found two other policy decisions made by the first drafters of the *Publication Manual* that have particular resonance today. First, the APA Council of Editors (1952) advised that negative or unexpected results were not to be accompanied by extended discussions: "Long 'alibis,' unsupported by evidence or sound theory, add nothing to the usefulness of the report" (p. 9). Second, this edition of the *Publication Manual* also stated that "sometimes space limitations dictate that the method be described synoptically in a journal, and a more detailed description be given in auxiliary publication (see sec. 5.)." (APA, Council of Editors, 1952, p. 9). This practice has rarely been used by journals but is now coming back into favor, as discussed throughout this volume.

In later editions of the *Publication Manual,* the APA recommendations for reporting became more detailed and specific. Of special note was the report of Wilkinson and the Task Force on Statistical Inference (1999), which presented guidelines for statistical reporting in APA journals. This report informed the content of the fourth edition of the *Publication Manual* (APA, 1994). Although the fifth edition did not contain an aggregated set of reporting standards, this does not mean that it was devoid of standards. Instead, prescriptions for reporting were embedded in various sections of the text. In the *Publication Manual*'s description of the parts of a manuscript, members of the JARS Group found statements regarding how to report and what to report in the Method and Results sections of a study (APA, 2001, pp. 10–29). For example, when discussing who participated in a study, the fifth edition stated, "When humans participated as the subjects of the study, report the procedures for selecting and assigning them and the agreements and payments made" (APA, 2001, p. 18). With regard to the Results section, the fifth edition stated, "Mention all relevant results, including those that run counter to the hypothesis" (APA, 2001, p. 20), and it provided descriptions of "sufficient statistics" (p. 23) that need to be reported.

So members of the JARS Group found that although reporting standards and requirements were not highlighted in the past editions of the *Publication Manual,* they appeared in it nonetheless. In that context, we concluded that the proposals we offered could be viewed not as breaking new ground for psychological research reporting but rather as systematizing, clarifying, and somewhat expanding standards that already existed. The intended contribution of our effort became one of increased emphasis as much as of increased content.

Drafting, Vetting, and Refining the JARS

After these initial explorations of existing reporting standards, members of the JARS Group canvassed the APA Council of Editors to find out the degree to which the CONSORT and TREND standards were already used in APA journals and to learn about other reporting standards. Then, we compared the content of the CONSORT, TREND, and AERA standards with one another and developed a combined list of non-redundant elements contained in any or all of the three sets of standards. Finally, we examined the combined list, rewrote some items so that they would better apply to the work of psychologists, and added a few suggestions of our own.

This combined list was then shared with the APA Council of Editors, the *Publication Manual* Revision Task Force, and the APA Publications and Communications Board. These groups were asked to react to the list. After receiving comments from the Board as well as anonymous reactions from reviewers chosen by the *American Psychologist,* we revised our report and arrived at the list of recommendations contained in Tables A1.1 through A1.3 and Figure A1.1. The report was then approved by the Publications and Communications Board.

Those of us in the JARS Group recognized that our work was incomplete because we included only one family of research designs. In the future, we hope (and expect) that new modules regarding other research designs will be added to the standards to be used in conjunction with Table A1.1. For example, to name just a few, modules could be constructed for the reporting of

- longitudinal studies with multiple data collection times;
- studies presenting structural equation models, which have a unique set of statistical procedures;
- regression discontinuity designs;
- single-case designs; and
- real-time data capture designs.

Also, additional standards could be adopted for any of the parts of a report. For example, the Evidence-Based Behavioral Medicine Committee (Davidson et al., 2003) examined each of the 22 items on the CONSORT checklist and described for each special considerations for reporting of research on behavioral medicine interventions. This committee also proposed an additional five items, not included in the CONSORT list, that they felt should be included in reports on behavioral medicine interventions.[2] The JARS Group encouraged other authoritative groups of interested researchers, practitioners, and journal editorial teams to use the JARS tables as a starting point in their efforts to create article standards and to add or delete items and modules to fit the information needs dictated by research designs that are prominent in their specific subdisciplines and topic areas. These revisions could then be incorporated into future iterations of the JARS. In this book, only the original tables are covered. In future editions, perhaps new tables will be added.

Other Issues Related to Reporting Standards

A Definition of *Reporting Standards*

The JARS Group struggled with the issue of how prescriptive our effort should be. We recognized that our standards could be taken at least three different ways: as recommendations, standards, or requirements. We were indeed recommending that certain information be reported in the research write-up. We also thought these recommendations could be viewed as standards, or at least as a beginning effort at developing standards, because we thought researchers who followed them more closely would produce documents of greater value or quality. The recommendations set a standard based on an integration of efforts by authoritative groups of researchers and editors. However, we did not want the proposed standards to be viewed as requirements. The methods used in the subdisciplines of psychology vary greatly. The critical information needed to assess the quality of research and to integrate it successfully with other related studies varies from method to method and by the context of the topic under consideration. We felt that calling these guidelines *standards* rather than *requirements* would give them the weight of authority while retaining flexibility for authors and editors to use them in the most efficacious fashion.

Benefits and Drawbacks of Reporting Standards

The general principle that guided the establishment of the JARS was to promote sufficient and transparent descriptions of a study's design, implementation, and findings. Complete reporting allows readers to make a clearer assessment of the strengths and weaknesses of a study. This permits the users of the evidence to judge more accurately the appropriate inferences and applications derivable from research findings.

Further, the existence of reporting standards could have a positive effect on the way research is conducted. For example, by setting a standard that attrition rates should be reported (see Figure A1.1), researchers may begin considering more concretely what acceptable levels of attrition might be and feel compelled to implement procedures meant to maximize the number of participants who complete a study.

---

[2]These items involved the training and supervision of treatment providers, patient and provider treatment allegiance, the manner of testing by the provider, the success of treatment delivery by the provider, and treatment adherence.

Finally, reporting standards can make it easier for other researchers to design and conduct replications and related studies. Standards help by providing more complete descriptions of previous study recipes. Complete reporting of the critical aspects of design and results enables researchers to figure out what caused the difference in outcomes when new studies do not replicate the results of older ones.

The JARS Group also thought it was important to point out that reporting standards also can have a downside. We tried to highlight the relationship between standards and standardization and why we were not interested in calling our effort "requirements." For example, standardized reporting could fill articles with details of methods and results that are inconsequential to interpretation. The critical facts about a study can get lost in an excess of minutiae. Also, a forced consistency can lead a researcher to ignore important uniqueness. We thought that reporting standards that appeared comprehensive might lead researchers to believe that if it is not asked for or does not conform to criteria specified in the standards, it is not necessary to report. This was not our intent. The standards you encounter in this book may appear exhaustive, but they should not lead you to omit information critical to understanding what was done in a study and what was found.

Again, the JARS Group noted that different methods are required for studying different psychological phenomena. What needs to be reported to evaluate the correspondence between methods and inferences is highly dependent on the research question and approach and the context in which the study is being conducted. Inferences about the effectiveness of psychotherapy, for example, require attention to aspects of research design and analysis that are different from those important for inferences in the neuroscience of text processing. This context dependency pertains not only to topic-specific considerations but also to research designs. Thus, an experimental study of the determinants of well-being analyzed with analysis of variance raises different reporting needs than does a study on the same topic that has a longitudinal design without an intervention using structural equation modeling.

Obstacles to Developing Standards

The first obstacle we ran into while developing the JARS was that differing taxonomies of research approaches exist and that different terms are used within different subdisciplines to describe the same research procedures. For example, researchers in health psychology typically refer to studies that use experimental manipulations of treatments conducted in naturalistic settings as *randomized clinical trials*, whereas similar designs are referred to as *randomized field trials* in educational psychology. As a further example, the terms *multilevel modeling, hierarchical linear modeling,* and *mixed-effects modeling* all are used to identify a similar approach to data analysis. To address the problem of terminology differences across the disciplines of social and behavioral sciences and the subdisciplines of psychology, we attempted to use the simplest descriptions possible and to avoid jargon in the JARS tables.

A second obstacle we encountered was that certain research topics and methods reveal different levels of consensus regarding what is and is not important to report. Generally, the newer and more complex the method, the less agreement there is about reporting standards. For example, although there are many benefits to reporting effect sizes, there are certain situations (e.g., multilevel designs) in which no clear consensus exists on how best to conceptualize and/or calculate effect-size measures. In a related vein, reporting a confidence interval with an effect size is sound advice. However, calculating confidence intervals for effect sizes is often difficult given the current state of software. For this reason, the JARS Group avoided developing reporting standards for research designs about which a professional consensus has not yet emerged. As consensus emerges, the JARS tables can be expanded with new modules.

Finally, the rapid pace of developments in methodology dictates that any standards would have to be updated frequently to remain relevant. For example, the state of the art for reporting various analytic techniques is in a constant state of flux. Although some general principles (e.g., reporting the estimation procedure used in a structural equation model) can incorporate new developments easily, other developments can involve fundamentally new types of data for which standards must, by necessity, evolve. New and emerging methods used in psychological research, such as functional neuroimaging and molecular genetics, may require frequent revision of standards to ensure that the current standards are covering what researchers in the field think is important.

Development of the MARS

Members of the JARS Group did the work of developing the MARS in much the same way as they developed the JARS. We began by contacting the members of the Society for Research Synthesis Methodology and asking them to share what they thought were the critical aspects of conducting a meta-analysis that needed to be reported so that readers could make informed, critical judgments about the appropriateness of the methods used for the inferences drawn. This query led to the identification of four other efforts to establish reporting standards for meta-analyses. These included the Quality of Reporting of Meta-Analysis Statement (Moher et al., 1999) and its revision, Preferred Reporting Items for Systematic Reviews and Meta-Analyses (PRISMA; Moher, Tetzlaff, Liberati, Altman, & the PRISMA Group, 2009), as well as the Meta-Analysis of Observational Studies in Epidemiology (Stroup et al., 2000) and the Potsdam Consultation on Meta-Analysis (Cook, Sackett, & Spitzer, 1995).

Next, members of the JARS Group compared the content of the four sets of standards with one another and developed a combined list of nonredundant elements. We then examined the combined list; rewrote some items for maximum applicability to the fields of psychological, social, and behavioral science; and added a few suggestions of our own. We shared the resulting recommendations with a subgroup of members of the Society for Research Synthesis Methodology who had experience writing and reviewing research syntheses in the discipline of psychology. After their suggestions were incorporated into the list, the items were shared with members of the APA Publications and Communications Board. We arrived at the list of recommendations contained in Table A6.1. These recommendations were then approved by the Publications and Communications Board.

Future Uses of JARS

The modular approach described in previous chapters makes it possible for other research designs to be added to the JARS. As these standards are developed, they can be given different module labels (our label is "Studies With an Experimental Manipulation or

Intervention") as well as their own submodules (in our case, "Studies Using Random Assignment" and "Studies Using Nonrandom Assignment"), depending on what is needed to fully capture the variations in that research design.

Members of the JARS Group recognize that our work is incomplete because we have included only one family of research designs. In the future, we plan to add new modules for other research designs that can be used in conjunction with Table A1.1. Also, additional standards could be adopted for any of the parts of a report (see, e.g., Davidson et al., 2003). Perhaps these will be added to future revisions of the JARS (and this book).

APPENDIX

Front Matter and Abstracts for the
14 Articles Used as Examples

Journal of Experimental Psychology:
Human Perception and Performance
2009, Vol. 35, No. 2, 520–529

© 2009 American Psychological Association
0096-1523/09/$12.00 DOI:10.1037/a0013552

Comprehension of Familiar and Unfamiliar Native Accents Under Adverse Listening Conditions

Patti Adank
Radboud University Nijmegen

Bronwen G. Evans
University College London

Jane Stuart-Smith
University of Glasgow

Sophie K. Scott
University College London

This study aimed to determine the relative processing cost associated with comprehension of an unfamiliar native accent under adverse listening conditions. Two sentence verification experiments were conducted in which listeners heard sentences at various signal-to-noise ratios. In Experiment 1, these sentences were spoken in a familiar or an unfamiliar native accent or in two familiar native accents. In Experiment 2, they were spoken in a familiar or unfamiliar native accent or in a nonnative accent. The results indicated that the differences between the native accents influenced the speed of language processing under adverse listening conditions and that this processing speed was modulated by the relative familiarity of the listener with the native accent. Furthermore, the results showed that the processing cost associated with the nonnative accent was larger than for the unfamiliar native accent.

Keywords: speech comprehension, native accents, nonnative accents, adverse listening conditions

Journal of Consulting and Clinical Psychology
2009, Vol. 77, No. 5, 961–973

© 2009 American Psychological Association
0022-006X/09/$12.00 DOI: 10.1037/a0016685

Attention Training in Individuals With Generalized Social Phobia: A Randomized Controlled Trial

Nader Amir
San Diego State University

Courtney Beard
Brown University

Charles T. Taylor
San Diego State University

Heide Klumpp
University of Michigan

Jason Elias
McLean Hospital

Michelle Burns
University of Georgia

Xi Chen
San Diego State University

The authors conducted a randomized, double-blind placebo-controlled trial to examine the efficacy of an attention training procedure in reducing symptoms of social anxiety in 44 individuals diagnosed with generalized social phobia (GSP). Attention training comprised a probe detection task in which pictures of faces with either a threatening or neutral emotional expression cued different locations on the computer screen. In the attention modification program (AMP), participants responded to a probe that always followed neutral faces when paired with a threatening face, thereby directing attention away from threat. In the attention control condition (ACC), the probe appeared with equal frequency in the position of the threatening and neutral faces. Results revealed that the AMP facilitated attention disengagement from threat from pre- to postassessment and reduced clinician- and self-reported symptoms of social anxiety relative to the ACC. The percentage of participants no longer meeting *Diagnostic and Statistical Manual of Mental Disorders* (4th ed.) criteria for GSP at postassessment was 50% in the AMP and 14% in the ACC. Symptom reduction in the AMP group was maintained during 4-month follow-up assessment. These results suggest that computerized attention training procedures may be beneficial for treating social phobia.

Keywords: social phobia, attention, treatment, information processing

A Quasi-Experimental Study on Management Coaching Effectiveness

Will. J. G. Evers, André Brouwers, and Welko Tomic
The Open University

Coaching has become an important managerial instrument of support. However, there is a lack of research on its effectiveness. The authors conducted a quasi-experimental study to figure out whether coaching really leads to presupposed individual goals. Sixty managers of the federal government were divided in 2 groups: one group followed a coaching program, the other did not. Before the coaching program started (Time 1), self-efficacy beliefs and outcome expectancies were measured, linked to 3 central domains of functioning: setting one's own goals, acting in a balanced way, and mindful living and working. Four months later (Time 2), the same variables were measured again. Results showed that the coached group scored significantly higher than the control group on 2 variables: outcome expectancies to act in a balanced way and self-efficacy beliefs to set one's own goals. Future examination might reveal whether coaching will also be effective among managers who work at different management levels, whether the effects found will be long-lasting, and whether subordinates experience differences in the way their manager functions before and after the coaching.

Keywords: management coaching, quasi-experiment, outcome experiences, self-efficacy

Copyright 2006 by the American Psychological Association and the Society of Consulting Psychology, 1065-9293/06/$12.00
DOI: 10.1037/1065-9293.58.3.174
Consulting Psychology Journal: Practice and Research, Vol. 58, No. 3, 174–182

Developmental Psychology
2009, Vol. 45, No. 5, 1389–1405

© 2009 American Psychological Association
0012-1649/09/$12.00 DOI: 10.1037/a0015210

Pathways to Paternal Engagement:
Longitudinal Effects of Risk and Resilience on Nonresident Fathers

Jay Fagan
Temple University

Rob Palkovitz
University of Delaware

Kevin Roy
University of Maryland

Danielle Farrie
Temple University

This article assesses the longitudinal effects of risk and resilience on unmarried nonresident fathers' engagement with children across the first 3 years of their lives. The authors used a subsample of 549 men from the Fragile Families and Child Wellbeing Study who were unmarried and noncohabiting at the time of the child's birth. They found not only that risk and resilience factors had a direct effect on paternal engagement but also that their association with engagement was mediated by fathers' continued nonresidence and mother–father relationship quality. Men who leave trajectories of high risk behind during the transition to fatherhood and who have a trajectory characterized by resilience factors are more likely to experience better relationships with the mother of their children, more likely to establish subsequent coresidence with their children, and more likely to remain involved in their children's lives on a daily basis. Implications for policy and programs serving fathers and families are discussed.

Keywords: fragile families, nonresident fathers, father involvement, resilience, risk

Journal of Experimental Psychology:
Learning, Memory, and Cognition
2009, Vol. 35, No. 5, 1105–1122

© 2009 American Psychological Association
0278-7393/09/$12.00 DOI: 10.1037/a0016548

Deficits in Cross-Race Face Learning:
Insights From Eye Movements and Pupillometry

Stephen D. Goldinger
Arizona State University

Yi He
Yale University

Megan H. Papesh
Arizona State University

The own-race bias (ORB) is a well-known finding wherein people are better able to recognize and discriminate own-race faces, relative to cross-race faces. In 2 experiments, participants viewed Asian and Caucasian faces, in preparation for recognition memory tests, while their eye movements and pupil diameters were continuously monitored. In Experiment 1 (with Caucasian participants), systematic differences emerged in both measures as a function of depicted race: While encoding cross-race faces, participants made fewer (and longer) fixations, they preferentially attended to different sets of features, and their pupils were more dilated, all relative to own-race faces. Also, in both measures, a pattern emerged wherein some participants reduced their apparent encoding effort to cross-race faces over trials. In Experiment 2 (with Asian participants), the authors observed the same patterns, although the ORB favored the opposite set of faces. Taken together, the results suggest that the ORB appears during initial perceptual encoding. Relative to own-race face encoding, cross-race encoding requires greater effort, which may reduce vigilance in some participants.

Keywords: face memory, own-race bias, eye movements, pupil dilation

Journal of Experimental Psychology:
Animal Behavior Processes
2009, Vol. 35, No. 4, 447–472

© 2009 American Psychological Association
0097-7403/09/$12.00 DOI: 10.1037/a0015626

The Dynamics of Conditioning and Extinction

Peter R. Killeen, Federico Sanabria, and Igor Dolgov
Arizona State University

Pigeons responded to intermittently reinforced classical conditioning trials with erratic bouts of responding to the conditioned stimulus. Responding depended on whether the prior trial contained a peck, food, or both. A linear persistence–learning model moved pigeons into and out of a response state, and a Weibull distribution for number of within-trial responses governed in-state pecking. Variations of trial and intertrial durations caused correlated changes in rate and probability of responding and in model parameters. A novel prediction—in the protracted absence of food, response rates can plateau above 0—was validated. The model predicted smooth acquisition functions when instantiated with the probability of food but a more accurate jagged learning curve when instantiated with trial-to-trial records of reinforcement. The Skinnerian parameter was dominant only when food could be accelerated or delayed by pecking. These experiments provide a framework for trial-by-trial accounts of conditioning and extinction that increases the information available from the data, permitting such accounts to comment more definitively on complex contemporary models of momentum and conditioning.

Keywords: autoshaping, behavioral momentum, classical conditioning, dynamic analyses, instrumental conditioning

Journal of Educational Psychology
2008, Vol. 100, No. 4, 741–753

Copyright 2008 by the American Psychological Association
0022-0663/08/$12.00 DOI: 10.1037/a0013099

Classroom Age Composition and Developmental Change in 70 Urban Preschool Classrooms

Arlen C. Moller
Children's Institute, Inc., and Gettysburg College

Emma Forbes-Jones and A. Dirk Hightower
Children's Institute, Inc., and University of Rochester

A multilevel modeling approach was used to investigate the influence of age composition in 70 urban preschool classrooms. A series of hierarchical linear models demonstrated that greater variance in classroom age composition was negatively related to development on the Child Observation Record (COR) Cognitive, Motor, and Social subscales. This was true when controlling for class size, general classroom quality, and socioeconomic status at the classroom level and for age, gender, and baseline ability at the child level. Additionally, to address possible concerns related to nonrandom assignment to classrooms, a series of models were run including variance in developmental age (i.e., baseline ability) at the classroom level and at the child level. The results were consistent for chronological age composition and developmental age composition at the classroom level; greater variance in classroom developmental age composition was negatively related to Time 2 scores on the COR Cognitive, Motor, and Social subscales. Furthermore, a cross-level interaction indicated that negative influence of greater variance in classroom developmental age composition was stronger for children older in developmental age. Implications for early childhood education policy are discussed.

Keywords: preschool, mixed age, single age, age composition, Child Observation Record

Health Psychology
2008, Vol. 27, No. 6, 799–810

Copyright 2008 by the American Psychological Association
0278-6133/08/$12.00 DOI: 10.1037/a0013105

Using the Internet to Assist Smoking Prevention and Cessation in Schools: A Randomized, Controlled Trial

Cameron D. Norman, Oonagh Maley,
and Xiaoqiang Li
University of Toronto

Harvey A. Skinner
York University

Objective: To evaluate the impact of a classroom-based, web-assisted tobacco intervention addressing smoking prevention and cessation with adolescents. *Design:* A 2-group randomized control trial with 1,402 male and female students in Grades 9 through 11 from 14 secondary schools in Toronto, Canada. Participants were randomly assigned to a tailored web-assisted tobacco intervention or an interactive control condition task conducted during a single classroom session with e-mail follow-up. The cornerstone of the intervention was a 5-stage interactive website called the *Smoking Zine* (http://www.smokingzine.org) integrated into a program that included a paper-based journal, a small group form of motivational interviewing, and tailored e-mails. *Main Outcome Measure:* Resistance to smoking, behavioral intentions to smoke, and cigarette use were assessed at baseline, postintervention, and 3- and 6-month follow-up. Multilevel logistic growth modeling was used to assess the effect of the intervention on change overtime. *Results:* The integrated *Smoking Zine* program helped smokers significantly reduce the likelihood of having high intentions to smoke and increased their likelihood of high resistance to continued cigarette use at 6 months. The intervention also significantly reduced the likelihood of heavy cigarette use adoption by nonsmokers during the study period. *Conclusion:* The *Smoking Zine* intervention provided cessation motivation for smokers most resistant to quitting at baseline and prevented nonsmoking adolescents from becoming heavy smokers at 6 months. By providing an accessible and attractive method of engaging young people in smoking prevention and cessation, this interactive and integrated program provides a novel vehicle for school- and population- level health promotion.

Keywords: Internet, smoking prevention, smoking cessation, adolescents, school-based interventions

Journal of Occupational Health Psychology
2009, Vol. 14, No. 3, 318–333

© 2009 American Psychological Association
1076-8998/09/$12.00 DOI: 10.1037/a0015852

Exploring Relationships Among Anger, Perceived Organizational Support, and Workplace Outcomes

Olivia A. O'Neill, Robert J. Vandenberg, David M. DeJoy, and Mark G. Wilson
University of Georgia

The present study examines anger within a perceived organizational support (POS) theory framework. Using structural equation modeling, the authors explored relationships among POS, anger, and workplace outcomes in a sample of 1,136 employees in 21 stores of a U.S. retail organization. At both individual and store levels, low POS was directly associated with greater anger. At the individual level, anger partially mediated relationships among low POS and turnover intentions, absences, and accidents on the job. Anger had direct and indirect effects on alcohol consumption and health-related risk taking. At the store level, anger had direct negative effects on inventory loss and turnover. The authors interpret these findings in light of social exchange theory and emotion regulation theory.

Keywords: anger, perceived organizational support, turnover, health, multilevel models

Journal of Personality and Social Psychology
2008, Vol. 95, No. 2, 293–307

Copyright 2008 by the American Psychological Association
0022-3514/08/$12.00 DOI: 10.1037/0022-3514.95.2.293

Why People Are Reluctant to Tempt Fate

Jane L. Risen
University of Chicago

Thomas Gilovich
Cornell University

The present research explored the belief that it is bad luck to "tempt fate." Studies 1 and 2 demonstrated that people do indeed have the intuition that actions that tempt fate increase the likelihood of negative outcomes. Studies 3–6 examined our claim that the intuition is due, in large part, to the combination of the automatic tendencies to attend to negative prospects and to use accessibility as a cue when judging likelihood. Study 3 demonstrated that negative outcomes are more accessible following actions that tempt fate than following actions that do not tempt fate. Studies 4 and 5 demonstrated that the heightened accessibility of negative outcomes mediates the elevated perceptions of likelihood. Finally, Study 6 examined the automatic nature of the underlying processes. The types of actions that are thought to tempt fate as well as the role of society and culture in shaping this magical belief are discussed.

Keywords: tempt fate, magical thinking, accessibility, negativity

Psychology of Addictive Behaviors
2009, Vol. 23, No. 3, 491–499

© 2009 American Psychological Association
0893-164X/09/$12.00 DOI: 10.1037/a0016632

Evidence for a Putative Biomarker for Substance Dependence

Jeanette Taylor and Lisa M. James
Florida State University

Electrodermal response modulation (ERM) reflects the reduction in skin conductance response to an aversive stimulus that is temporally predictable relative to when it is unpredictable. Poor ERM is associated with substance dependence (SD). It was hypothesized that ERM is a putative biomarker for SD rather than for externalizing disorders generally. Participants included 83 controls (no SD, antisocial personality disorder [PD] or borderline PD), 52 participants with SD only (SD and no PD), 12 with PD only (antisocial and/or borderline PD and no SD), and 35 comorbid (having SD and PD). Diagnoses at definite and probable certainty levels were used and were determined by semistructured clinical interviews. ERM was calculated from skin conductance responses to predictable and unpredictable 2-s 110-dB white noise blasts. As expected, the SD-only and comorbid groups had significantly lower ERM scores than the control group, which did not differ significantly from the PD-only group. Results provide preliminary evidence that ERM is a putative biomarker for SD. Future research should examine cognitive correlates of ERM in an effort to understand why it relates to SD.

Keywords: electrodermal response, substance dependence, antisocial personality disorder, borderline personality disorder, disinhibition

Rehabilitation Psychology
2009, Vol. 54, No. 3, 299–305

© 2009 American Psychological Association
0090-5550/09/$12.00 DOI: 10.1037/a0016807

The Relationship Between Employment-Related Self-Efficacy and Quality of Life Following Traumatic Brain Injury

Theodore Tsaousides, Adam Warshowsky, Teresa A. Ashman, Joshua B. Cantor, Lisa Spielman, and Wayne A. Gordon
Mount Sinai School of Medicine

Objectives: This study examines the relative contribution of employment-related and general self-efficacy to perceptions of quality of life (QoL) for individuals with traumatic brain injury. *Design:* Correlational. *Setting:* Community-based research and training center. *Participants:* 427 individuals with self-reported TBI under the age of 65 were included in analysis. *Main Outcome Measure:* Employment-related self-efficacy, general self-efficacy, perceived quality of life (PQoL), unmet important needs (UIN). *Results:* Significant correlations were found between income, injury severity, age at injury, and employment and the QoL variables. In addition, employment-related and general self-efficacy correlated positively with both PQoL and UIN. Employment-related and general self-efficacy accounted for 16% of the variance in PQoL and 9.5% of the variance in UIN, over and above other variables traditionally associated with QoL. *Conclusions:* These findings highlight the importance of including subjective appraisals of employment, such as perceived self-efficacy at the workplace, in assessing QoL and successful return to work following TBI.

Keywords: traumatic brain injury, employment, self-efficacy, quality of life

Journal of Educational Psychology
2008, Vol. 100, No. 2, 272–290

Copyright 2008 by the American Psychological Association
0022-0663/08/$12.00 DOI: 10.1037/0022-0663.100.2.272

Repeated Reading Intervention: Outcomes and Interactions With Readers' Skills and Classroom Instruction

Patricia F. Vadasy and Elizabeth A. Sanders
Washington Research Institute

This study examined effects of a repeated reading intervention, *Quick Reads*, with incidental word-level scaffolding instruction. Second- and 3rd-grade students with passage-reading fluency performance between the 10th and 60th percentiles were randomly assigned to dyads, which were in turn randomly assigned to treatment (paired tutoring, $n = 82$) or control (no tutoring, $n = 80$) conditions. Paraeducators tutored dyads for 30 min per day, 4 days per week, for 15 weeks (November–March). At midintervention, most teachers with students in the study were formally observed during their literacy blocks. Multilevel modeling was used to test for direct treatment effects on pretest–posttest gains as well as to test for unique treatment effects after classroom oral text reading time, 2 pretests, and corresponding interactions were accounted for. Model results revealed both direct and unique treatment effects on gains in word reading and fluency. Moreover, complex interactions between group, oral text reading time, and pretests were also detected, suggesting that pretest skills should be taken into account when considering repeated reading instruction for 2nd and 3rd graders with low to average passage-reading fluency.

Keywords: multilevel modeling, fluency, repeated reading, verbal efficiency, paraeducators

Psychotherapy Theory, Research, Practice, Training
2009, Vol. 46, No. 3, 362–375

© 2009 American Psychological Association
0033-3204/09/$12.00 DOI: 10.1037/a0017002

Do Personality Problems Improve During Psychodynamic Supportive–Expressive Psychotherapy? Secondary Outcome Results From a Randomized Controlled Trial for Psychiatric Outpatients With Personality Disorders

Bo Vinnars and
Barbro Thormählen
Karolinska Institutet

Robert Gallop
West Chester University

Kristina Norén
Karolinska Institutet

Jacques P. Barber
University of Pennsylvania School
of Medicine

Studies involving patients with personality disorders (PDs) have not focused on improvement of core aspects of the PD. The authors examined changes in quality of object relations, interpersonal problems, psychological mindedness, and personality traits in a sample of 156 patients with *Diagnostic and Statistical Manual of Mental Disorders* (4th ed.) PD diagnoses being randomized to either manualized or nonmanualized dynamic psychotherapy. Effect sizes adjusted for symptomatic change and reliable change indices were calculated. The authors found that both treatments were equally effective at reducing personality pathology. Only in neuroticism did the nonmanualized group do better during the follow-up period. The largest improvement was found in quality of object relations. For the remaining variables, only small and clinically insignificant magnitudes of change were found.

Keywords: personality disorder, psychodynamic psychotherapy, psychotherapy outcome, personality problems

References

Adank, P., Evans, B. G., Stuart-Smith, J., & Scott, S. K. (2009). Comprehension of familiar and unfamiliar native accents under adverse listening conditions. *Journal of Experimental Psychology: Human Perception and Performance, 35,* 520–529. doi:10.1037/a0013552

Altman, D. G., Schulz, K. F., Moher, D., Egger, M., Davidoff, F., Elbourne, D., . . . Lang, T. (2001). The revised CONSORT statement for reporting randomized trials: Explanation and elaboration. *Annals of Internal Medicine, 134,* 663–694.

American Educational Research Association. (2006). Standards for reporting on empirical social science research in AERA publications. *Educational Researcher, 35*(6), 33–40. doi:10.3102/0013189X035006033

American Psychological Association. (1994). *Publication manual of the American Psychological Association* (4th ed.). Washington, DC: Author.

American Psychological Association. (2001). *Publication manual of the American Psychological Association* (5th ed.). Washington, DC: Author.

American Psychological Association. (2010a). *Ethical principles of psychologists and code of conduct (2002, amended June 1, 2010).* Retrieved from http://www.apa.org /ethics/code/index.aspx

American Psychological Association. (2010b). *Publication manual of the American Psychological Association* (6th ed.). Washington, DC: Author.

American Psychological Association, Council of Editors. (1952). Publication manual of the American Psychological Association. *Psychological Bulletin, 49*(Suppl., Pt. 2), 389–449.

American Psychological Association, Presidential Task Force on Evidence-Based Practice. (2006). Evidence-based practice in psychology. *American Psychologist, 61,* 271–285. doi:10.1037/0003-066X.61.4.271

Amir, N., Beard, C., Taylor, C. T., Klumpp, H., Elias, J., Burns, M., & Chen, X. (2009). Attention training in individuals with generalized social phobia: A randomized controlled trial. *Journal of Consulting and Clinical Psychology, 77,* 961–973. doi:10.1037/a0016685

APA Publications and Communications Board Working Group on Journal Article Reporting Standards. (2008). Reporting standards for research in psychology: Why do we need them? What might they be? *American Psychologist, 63,* 839–851. doi:10.1037/0003-066X.63.9.839

Borenstein, M. (2009). Effect sizes for studies with continuous data. In H. Cooper, L. V. Hedges, & J. C. Valentine (Eds.), *The handbook of research synthesis and meta-analysis* (2nd ed., pp. 221–236). New York, NY: Russell Sage Foundation.

Borenstein, M., Hedges, L. V., Higgins, J. P. T., & Rothstein, H. R. (2009). *Introduction to meta-analysis.* doi:10.1002/9780470743386

Boruch, R. F. (1997). *Randomized experiments for planning and evaluation: A practical guide.* Thousand Oaks, CA: Sage.

Bricker, J. B., Rajan, K. B., Zalewski, M., Andersen, M. R., Ramey, M., & Peterson, A. V. (2009). Psychological and social risk factors in adolescent smoking transitions: A population-based longitudinal study. *Health Psychology, 28,* 439–447. doi:10.1037/a0014568

Burgmans, S., van Boxtel, M. P. J., Vuurman, E. F. P. M., Smeets, F., Gronenschild, E. H. B. M., Uylings, H. B. M., & Jolles, J. (2009). The prevalence of cortical gray matter atrophy may be overestimated in the healthy aging brain. *Neuropsychology, 23,* 541–550. doi:10.1037/a0016161

Centers for Disease Control and Prevention. (2009). *Transparent reporting of evaluations with nonexperimental designs (TREND).* Retrieved from http://www.cdc.gov /trendstatement/

Cohen, J. (1988). *Statistical power analysis for the behavioral sciences* (2nd ed.). Hillsdale, NJ: Erlbaum.

Collins, L. (1977). A name to conjure with. *European Journal of Marketing, 11,* 340–363.

Consolidated Standards of Reporting Trials. (2007). *CONSORT: Strength in science, sound ethics.* Retrieved from http://www.consort-statement.org/

Cook, D. J., Sackett, D. L., & Spitzer, W. O. (1995). Methodologic guidelines for systematic reviews of randomized control trials in health care from the Potsdam Consultation on Meta-Analysis. *Journal of Clinical Epidemiology, 48,* 167–171. doi:10.1016/0895-4356(94)00172-M

Cooper, H. (2006). Research questions and research designs. In P. A. Alexander, P. H. Winne, & G. Phye (Eds.), *Handbook of research in educational psychology* (2nd ed., pp. 849–877). Mahwah, NJ: Erlbaum.

Cooper, H. (2010). *Research synthesis and meta-analysis: A step-by-step approach* (4th ed.). Thousand Oaks, CA: Sage.

Cooper, H., DeNeve, K., & Charlton, K. (1997). Finding the missing science: The fate of studies submitted for review by a human subjects committee. *Psychological Methods, 2,* 447–452. doi:10.1037/1082-989X.2.4.447

Cooper, H., & Dent, A. (2011). Ethical issues in the conduct and reporting of meta-analysis. In A. T. Panter & S. K. Sterba (Eds.), *Handbook of ethics in quantitative methodology* (pp. 417–444). New York, NY: Routledge.

Cooper, H., Hedges, L. V., & Valentine, J. C. (Eds.). (2009). *The handbook of research synthesis and meta-analysis* (2nd ed.). New York, NY: Russell Sage Foundation.

Davidson, K. W., Goldstein, M., Kaplan, R. M., Kaufmann, P. G., Knatterud, G. L., Orleans, T. C., . . . Whitlock, E. P. (2003). Evidence-based behavioral medicine: What is it and how do we achieve it? *Annals of Behavioral Medicine, 26,* 161–171. doi:10.1207/S15324796ABM2603_01

Evers, W. J. G., Brouwers, A., & Tomic, W. (2006). A quasi-experimental study on management coaching effectiveness. *Consulting Psychology Journal: Practice and Research, 58,* 174–182. doi:10.1037/1065-9293.58.3.174

Fagan, J., Palkovitz, R., Roy, K., & Farrie, D. (2009). Pathways to paternal engagement: Longitudinal effects of risk and resilience on nonresident fathers. *Developmental Psychology, 45,* 1389–1405. doi:10.1037/a0015210

Fleiss, J. L., & Berlin, J. A. (2009). Measures of effect size for categorical data. In H. Cooper, L. V. Hedges, & J. C. Valentine (Eds.), *The handbook of research synthesis and meta-analysis* (2nd ed., pp. 237–253). New York, NY: Russell Sage Foundation.

Gleser, L. J., & Olkin, I. (2009). Stochastically dependent effect sizes. In H. Cooper, L. V. Hedges, & J. C. Valentine (Eds.), *The handbook of research synthesis and meta-analysis* (2nd ed., pp. 357–376). New York, NY: Russell Sage Foundation.

Goldinger, S. D., He, Y., & Papesh, M. H. (2009). Deficits in cross-race face learning: Insights from eye movements and pupillometry. *Journal of Experimental Psychology: Learning, Memory, and Cognition, 35,* 1105–1122. doi:10.1037/a0016548

Grabe, S., Ward, L. M., & Hyde, J. S. (2008). The role of media in body image concerns among women: A meta-analysis of experimental and correlational studies. *Psychological Bulletin, 134,* 460–476. doi:10.1037/0033-2909.134.3.460

Grissom, R. J., & Kim, J. J. (2005). *Effect sizes for research: A broad practical approach.* Mahwah, NJ: Erlbaum.

Hedges, L. V. (1981). Distribution theory for Glass' estimator of effect size and related estimators. *Journal of Educational Statistics, 6,* 107–128. doi:10.2307/1164588

Hedges, L. V., & Vevea, J. L. (1998). Fixed- and random-effects models in meta-analysis. *Psychological Methods, 3,* 486–504. doi:10.1037/1082-989x.3.4.486

International Committee of Medical Journal Editors. (2007). *Uniform requirements for manuscripts submitted to biomedical journals: Writing and editing for biomedical publications.* Retrieved from http://www.icmje.org/#clin_trials

Killeen, P. R., Sanabria, F., & Dolgov, I. (2009). The dynamics of conditioning and extinction. *Journal of Experimental Psychology: Animal Behavior Processes, 35,* 447–472. doi:10.1037/a0015626

Kline, T. J. B. (2005). *Psychological testing: A practical approach to design and evaluation.* Thousand Oaks, CA: Sage.

Kohli, C. S., Harich, K. R., & Leuthesser, L. (2005). Creating brand identity: A study of evaluation of new brand names. *Journal of Business Research, 58,* 1506–1515. doi:10.1016/j.jbusres.2004.07.007

Lachin, J. M. (2005). A review of methods for futility stopping based on conditional power. *Statistics in Medicine, 24,* 2747–2764. doi:10.1002/sim.2151

Lipsey, M. W., & Wilson, D. B. (1993). The efficacy of psychological, educational, and behavioral treatment: Confirmation from meta-analysis. *American Psychologist, 48,* 1181–1209. doi:10.1037/0003-066X.48.12.1181

Little, R. J., Long, Q., & Lin, X. (2009). A comparison of methods for estimating the causal effect of a treatment in randomized clinical trials subject to noncompliance. *Biometrics, 65,* 640–649. doi:10.1111/j.1541-0420.2008.01066.x

Little, R. J., & Rubin, D. B. (2002). *Statistical analysis with missing data* (2nd ed.). Hoboken, NJ: Wiley.

Luke, D. A. (2004). *Multilevel modeling.* Thousand Oaks, CA: Sage.

McLanahan, S., & Garfinkel, I. (2000). *The Fragile Families and Child Wellbeing Study: Questions, design, and a few preliminary results* (Center for Research on Child Wellbeing Working Paper No. 00–07). Retrieved from http://crcw.princeton .edu/workingpapers/WP00-07-FF-McLanahan.pdf

Menard, S. (2002). *Applied logistic regression analysis* (2nd ed.). Thousand Oaks, CA: Sage.

Moher, D., Cook, D. J., Eastwood, S., Olkin, I., Rennie, D., Stroup, D., & the QUOROM Group. (1999). Improving the quality of reporting of meta-analysis of randomised controlled trials: The QUOROM statement. *The Lancet, 354,* 1896–1900. doi: 10.1016/S0140-6736(99)04149-5

Moher, D., Schulz, K. F., & Altman, D. G. (2001). The CONSORT statement: Revised recommendations for improving the quality of reports of parallel-group randomized trials. *Annals of Internal Medicine, 134,* 657–662.

Moher, D., Tetzlaff, J., Liberati, A., Altman, D. G., & the PRISMA Group. (2009). Preferred reporting items for systematic reviews and meta-analysis: The PRISMA statement. *PLoS Medicine, 6*(7), e1000097. doi:10.1371/journal.pmed.1000097

Moller, A. C., Forbes-Jones, E., & Hightower, A. D. (2008). Classroom age composition and developmental change in 70 urban preschool classrooms. *Journal of Educational Psychology, 100,* 741–753. doi:10.1037/a0013099

Muthén, L. K., & Muthén, B. O. (2006). *Mplus user's guide* (4th ed.). Los Angeles, CA: Author.

No Child Left Behind Act of 2001, Pub. L. No. 107-110, 115 Stat. 1425 (2002).

Norman, C. D., Maley, O., Li, X., & Skinner, H. A. (2008). Using the Internet to assist smoking prevention and cessation in schools: A randomized, controlled trial. *Health Psychology, 27,* 799–810.

O'Neill, O. A., Vandenberg, R. J., DeJoy, D. M., & Wilson, M. G. (2009). Exploring relationships among anger, perceived organizational support, and workplace outcomes. *Journal of Occupational Health Psychology, 14,* 318–333. doi:10.1037 /a0015852

Pocock, S. J. (2007). Statistical and ethical issues in monitoring clinical trials. *Statistics in Medicine, 12,* 1459–1469. doi:10.1002/sim.4780121512

Risen, J. L., & Gilovich, T. (2008). Why people are reluctant to tempt fate. *Journal of Personality and Social Psychology, 95,* 293–307. doi:10.1037/0022-3514.95.2.293

Sackett, D. L., Rosenberg, W. M. C., Gray, J. A. M., Haynes, R. B., & Richardson, W. S. (1996). Evidence based medicine: What it is and what it isn't. *British Medical Journal, 312,* 71–72.

Shadish, W. R., Cook, T. D., & Campbell, D. T. (2002). *Experimental and quasi-experimental designs for generalized causal inference.* Boston, MA: Houghton Mifflin.

Stroup, D. F., Berlin, J. A., Morton, S. C., Olkin, I., Williamson, G. D., Rennie, D., . . . Thacker, S. B. (2000). Meta-analysis of observational studies in epidemiology. *JAMA, 283,* 2008–2012. doi:10.1001/jama.283.15.2008

Taylor, J., & James, L. M. (2009). Evidence for a putative biomarker for substance dependence. *Psychology of Addictive Behaviors, 23,* 491–499. doi:10.1037/a0016632

Tsaousides, T., Warshowsky, A., Ashman, T. A., Cantor, J. B., Spielman, L., & Gordon, W. A. (2009). The relationship between employment-related self-efficacy and quality of life following traumatic brain injury. *Rehabilitation Psychology, 54,* 299–305. doi:10.1037/a0016807

Vadasy, P. F., & Sanders, E. A. (2008). Repeated reading intervention: Outcomes and interactions with readers' skills and classroom instruction. *Journal of Educational Psychology, 100,* 272–290. doi:10.1037/0022-0663.100.2.272

Vinnars, B., Thormählen, B., Gallop, R., Norén, K., & Barber, J. P. (2009). Do personality problems improve during psychodynamic supportive–expressive psychotherapy? Secondary outcome results from a randomized controlled trial for psychiatric outpatients with personality disorders. *Psychotherapy: Theory, Research, Practice, Training, 46,* 362–375. doi:10.1037/a0017002

Wheatley, K., & Clayton, D. (2003). Be skeptical about unexpected large apparent treatment effects: The case of an MRC AML12 randomization. *Controlled Clinical Trials, 24,* 66–70. doi:10.1016/S0197-2456(02)00273-8

Wilkinson, L., & the Task Force on Statistical Inference. (1999). Statistical methods in psychology journals: Guidelines and explanations. *American Psychologist, 54,* 594–604. doi:10.1037/0003-066X.54.8.594

Index

A

Abstracts, 7, 14, 18–20, 103
Acknowledgments, 17
Adank, P., 37–40, 42–44, 58, 60–61, 76–78
Adherence, 43–44
Adverse events, 9, 71
AERA. *See* American Educational Research Association
Alternative explanations, 101
American Educational Research Association (AERA), 107, 109
Amir, N., 32, 49–52, 57, 60, 69, 70, 81, 84–86
Andersen, M. R., 19
Animals, 29
APA Ethics Code, 15–17, 53–54
Assignment of participants
    in randomized field or clinical trials, 46–49
    recommendations for reporting on, 10
    in results section, 71
    statistical methods for, 51–52
Assumptions, 58
Attrition, 5
    differential, 46n9, 56
    rates of, 110
    in results section, 56–57
Author note, 15–18, 29

B

Barber, J. P., 37, 67, 88
Baseline data, 9, 69–70
Behavioral medicine interventions, 109–110
Bias, 78, 96
Biometric properties, 35–36
Blinding, 49
Bricker, J. B., 18–20
Brouwers, A., 47–48, 76
Burgmans, S., 19, 20

C

Campbell Collaboration, 106
Causality, 70, 80, 88
CDC (Centers for Disease Control), 107
Cells, 61–63
Centers for Disease Control (CDC), 107
Characteristics
    biometric properties, 35–36
    clinical, 69–70
    demographic, 28, 69–70
    in meta-analyses, 93–94
    of participants, 24–26, 87
    reporting in table, 28
    of studies in meta-analyses, 99

About the Author

Harris Cooper, PhD, is professor and chair of the Department of Psychology and Neuroscience at Duke University in Durham, North Carolina. He is known for his work in research synthesis and research methodology. His book *Research Synthesis and Meta-Analysis: A Step-by-Step Approach* (2010) is in its fourth edition. He is the coeditor of the *Handbook of Research Synthesis and Meta-Analysis* (2nd ed., 2009). In 2007, Dr. Cooper was appointed to membership on the National Academy of Sciences' Standing Committee on Social Science Research and Evidentiary Standards.

Dr. Cooper is also interested in the application of social and developmental psychology to educational policy issues. In particular, he studies how time on academic activities influences achievement. His topics of interest include homework, summer learning loss and summer school, year-round school calendars, extended school days and years, and full-day kindergarten.

From 2003 through mid-2009, Dr. Cooper served as editor of *Psychological Bulletin*. In 2007–2008, he also served on the committee that revised the *Publication Manual of the American Psychological Association*. In 2009, Dr. Cooper became the chief editorial advisor for the American Psychological Association's (APA's) journal publishing program. In this role he serves as a resource for the editors of APA journals as well as the mediator of disputes between editors and authors and between authors and authors. In addition, Dr. Cooper is editor-in-chief of APA's three-volume *Handbook of Research Methods in Psychology* slated for publication in 2012.